Is There a Duty to Obey the Law?

The central question in political philosophy is whether political states have the right to coerce their constituents and whether citizens have a moral duty to obey the commands of their state. Christopher Heath Wellman and A. John Simmons defend opposing answers to this question. Wellman bases his argument on samaritan obligations to perform easy rescues, arguing that each of us has a moral duty to obey the law as his or her fair share of the communal samaritan chore of rescuing our compatriots from the perils of the state of nature. Simmons counters that this and all other attempts to explain our duty to obey the law fail. Concentrating especially on refuting Natural Duty accounts of the duty to obey, he ultimately defends the view that there is no strong moral presumption in favor of obedience to or compliance with any existing state.

Christopher Heath Wellman is Associate Professor of Philosophy at Washington University in St. Louis. He works in ethics, specializing in political and legal philosophy, and he is the author of *A Theory of Secession: The Case for Political Self-Determination*.

A. John Simmons is Commonwealth Professor of Philosophy and Professor of Law at the University of Virginia. He is an editor of the journal *Philosophy & Public Affairs* and the author of several books, most recently *Justification and Legitimacy*.

D1054044

For and Against

General Editor: R. G. Frey

For and Against offers a new and exciting approach to the investigation of complex philosophical ideas and their impact on the way we think about a host of contemporary moral, social, and political issues. Two philosophical essays explore a topic of intense public interest from opposing points of view. This approach provides the reader with a balanced perspective on the topic; it also introduces the deep philosophical conflicts that underpin the differing views. The result is both a series of important statements on some of the most challenging questions facing our society and an introduction to moral, social, and political philosophy. Each essay is compact and nontechnical, yet avoids a simplistic, journalistic presentation of the topic.

Other books in the series:

David Schmidtz and Robert E. Goodin, *Social Welfare and Individual Responsibility*

Gerald Dworkin, R. G. Frey, and Sissela Bok, *Euthanasia and Physician-Assisted Suicide*

Douglas Husak and Peter de Marneffe, *The Legalization of Drugs*

Is There a Duty to Obey the Law?

Christopher Heath Wellman
Washington University in St. Louis

and

A. John Simmons
University of Virginia

CAMBRIDGE
UNIVERSITY PRESS

CAMBRIDGE UNIVERSITY PRESS
Cambridge, New York, Melbourne, Madrid, Cape Town, Singapore,
São Paulo, Delhi, Dubai, Tokyo, Mexico City

Cambridge University Press
The Edinburgh Building, Cambridge CB2 8RU, UK

Published in the United States of America by Cambridge University Press, New York

www.cambridge.org
Information on this title: www.cambridge.org/9780521537841

First published 2005

A catalogue record for this publication is available from the British Library

Library of Congress Cataloguing in Publication Data

Wellman, Christopher Heath.
Is there a duty to obey the law? / Christopher Heath Wellman, A. John Simmons.
     p.   cm. – (For and against)
ISBN 0-521-83097-4 (hardback) – ISBN 0-521-53784-3 (pbk.)
1. Law and ethics. 2. Political ethics. 3. Duty. I. Simmons, A. John (Alan John),
1950– II. Title. III. Series: For and against (Cambridge, England)
BJ55.W45 2006
172´.1 – dc22   2004028547

ISBN 978-0-521-83097-3 Hardback
ISBN 978-0-521-53784-1 Paperback

Contents

General Editor's Preface

SINCE the mid-1960s, the application of ethical theory to moral, social, political, and legal issues has formed a growing part of public life and of the philosophical curriculum. Except perhaps during the 1950s and the flowering of ordinary language philosophy, moral philosophers have always to some extent been concerned with the practical application of their theories. On the whole, however, they did little more than sketch implications or draw provisional conclusions with regard to practical issues based upon some distant familiarity with a few empirical facts. Today, the opposite is the case: They have come to immerse themselves in the subject matter of the issues with which they are normatively concerned, whether these come from law, medicine, business, or the affairs of social and political life. As a result, they have come to apply their theories with a much broader and deeper understanding of the factual setting within which the issues in question arise and have become of public concern.

Courses in applied ethics now figure throughout the philosophical curriculum, including, increasingly, within philosophy components of professional education. More and more periodicals – philosophical, professional, popular – devote space to medical and business ethics, to environmental and animal rights issues, to discussions of suicide, euthanasia, and physician-assisted suicide, to surrogate motherhood and the rights of children, to the ethics of war and the moral case for and against assisting famine victims, and so on. Indeed, new periodicals are devoted entirely to applied issues, from numerous environmental quarterlies to the vast number of journals in medical ethics that today feature a compendium of philosophical, medical, and sometimes popular authors writing on a diverse array of issues ultimately concerned with life, quality of life, and death.

What is striking about the *best* philosophical writing in all these areas (I concede that there is much chaff amongst the wheat) is that it is factually informed and methodologically situated in the subject areas under discussion to a degree that enables specialists in those areas – be they doctors, lawyers, environmentalists, or the like – to see the material as both engaging and relevant. Yet, the writing is pitched at the level of the educated person, comparatively free of technicalities and jargon, and devoted to matters of public concern. Much of it, whether by philosophers or others, such as economists and political and social scientists, is known outside the academy and has had the effect, as it were, of taking philosophy into the public arena.

Interest in applied ethics will continue to grow as a result of technological/scientific developments, enacted social policies, and political/economic decisions. For example, genetic engineering raises a number of important moral issues, from those that concern human cloning, illnesses, and treatments to those that center on alteration in animal species and the "creation" of new animals. Fetal tissue research holds out the promise of help for diabetics and those with Parkinson's disease, but even using the tissue, quite apart from how we acquire it, is a controversial affair. Equally contentious is the bringing to term of severely deformed fetuses who will die almost at once, in order to use their organs for transplant. But so, too, is xenography, or cross-species transplantation, in which animals are treated as repositories of organs for humans.

Social, political, and legal decisions always spur ethical interest. Topics such as obscenity, pornography, and censorship are of perennial interest, as are straightforwardly economic/political issues to do with capital punishment, equality, majoritarian democracy, the moral assessment of capitalism, and the provision of societal welfare. Today, some comparatively new issues have come to figure in this ethical landscape, from the place of children in society and all manner of interest in educational policy and practice to population policy and its relation to the distribution of various societal resources. And it is obvious that, throughout the world, issues to do with nationalism, political and judicial sovereignty, and immigration are of massive interest to educated persons and raise all kinds of moral questions.

This new series, For and Against, aims to cover a good many of these applied issues. Collectively, the volumes will form a kind of library of applied ethics.

Philosophy is an argumentative discipline: Among its best practitioners, whom this series will feature, it proceeds by the clear and careful articulation, analysis, and assessment of arguments. Clashes of arguments, ideas, principles, positions, and theories are its very lifeblood. The idea behind the series is very simple: It is to capture this clash. Two or more philosophers, in opposition on some moral, social, or political issue, will state and defend their positions on the issue in as direct and powerful a manner as they can. Theory will be involved, but the general aim is not to have two authors differ over the development or worth of a philosophical theory. Rather, it is to show the application of philosophy to practice, with each author using as much theory as he or she thinks necessary to state and defend his or her position on the topic. Educated people generally should be able to read and assess the success of the authors.

The volumes will be polemical but in the best sense: Each author will dispute and defend a position on some controversial matter by means of clear and careful argument. The end, obviously, is that each volume will exhibit to the full the best case each author can muster for his or her respective side to the controversy.

The central question the present volume addresses, one as old as philosophy itself, is whether there is an obligation to obey the law. The question is not whether a legal system does internally, as it were, demand that those subject to it obey its edicts; in some sense, all legal systems do this. The question, rather, is whether there are good moral reasons to do what the legal system requires of us and what society as a whole expects of us. What is the nature of those reasons? Are they persuasive? What are the underlying concerns of moral and political life that lead us to think that obedience to law is required of us? Does the notion of being a good citizen, a participating member of political society, require us to obey? And if we give a provisional answer in the affirmative, that, for example, to be good citizens we are at least provisionally obliged to obey the law, what kinds of qualifications do we acknowledge as affecting the issue of whether we are bound? Christopher Wellman argues that there is a provisional moral duty to obey the law. A. John Simmons argues that there is not. In a lively debate, conducted in clear and careful prose, these distinguished philosophers come to grips with the various facets of this issue, factual, moral, and political, in a way that should enable readers at the end to make up their minds about whether there is a duty to obey the law.

R. G. Frey

Acknowledgments

WE are immensely grateful to the many friends and colleagues who have helped shape our thinking on the duty to obey the law, and here we would like to express our gratitude to the anonymous readers who reviewed our preliminary proposal, as well as those who generously supplied written comments on earlier drafts of this book. In particular, John wishes to thank Nancy Schauber (and his daughter, Sarah, who was wonderfully tolerant of her working father), and Kit is indebted to David Lefkowitz and Carl Wellman. In addition, Kit is grateful to the National Endowment for the Humanities for a fellowship that enabled him to work on this project.

For their considerable help in preparing this book for publication, we are appreciative of all the highly skilled people with Cambridge University Press, especially Beatrice Rehl, Helen Wheeler, and Helen Greenberg. We are particularly indebted to Ray Frey, the series editor, for his sage advice and unfailing support at every stage of this project. Finally, it is with great sadness that we remember Terry Moore, the editor under whom this book was initiated. Terry was not only a distinguished editor; he was a consummate gentleman and a joy to work with. The profession is much poorer for his absence.

A. John Simmons
Christopher Heath Wellman

I Samaritanism and the Duty to Obey the Law

Christopher Heath Wellman

1   Why I Am Not an Anarchist

I don't have many vivid memories from childhood, but among those that stand out, I distinctly remember sitting at a stoplight and seeing a bumper sticker that proclaimed "Taxation is slavery!" This sticker made a great impression on me because I found it so bewildering; I could not fathom why anyone would compare *taxation* – a natural and appropriate part of our lives – to *slavery* – a horribly unjust institution. Indeed, at the time (I think I was about ten), I positively *looked forward* to the day when I would pay taxes. This may sound farfetched, but I was in awe of all that the state accomplished. In particular, I used to sit in the car and marvel at the incredible network of roads; I remember being amazed that people were able collectively to build such an extensive system of streets by merely pooling a portion of their individual incomes. Thus, I looked forward to paying my taxes principally because I wanted to share in the credit for what I considered a monumental communal achievement.

Probably because I thought it was too outlandish to be explained, I did not ask my father why anyone would compare taxation to slavery. As a consequence, it was not until many years later that I finally understood the point of the bumper sticker.[1] Taxation and slavery are alike insofar as both involve others nonconsensually taking at least a portion of the fruits of one's labor. Just

---

1 The "light bulb" moment occurred for me the summer after my first year of graduate school when I had the good fortune to hear a series of lectures by the extremely compelling anarcho-libertarian Randy Barnett.

as a slave owner essentially puts a gun to the heads of her slaves and forces them to work, the state essentially puts a gun to the heads of its constituents and demands that they hand over some of their wealth. Indeed, not only does the state coerce its constituents, it forcibly helps itself to a portion of their money in order to finance its continued coercion. Thus, if a government takes a third of one's income, for instance, then there is a very real sense in which the state appears morally tantamount to a slave owner who enslaves her slaves for only a third of their working lives.[2]

Although it might initially seem ludicrous to compare citizenship to slavery, upon closer inspection it proves surprisingly difficult to show why this comparison is inapt. One might protest that citizenship is importantly distinct from slavery insofar as the former is consensual, but the truth is that widespread political consent is a fiction.[3] Governments could not function effectively without uniformly coercing virtually everyone within their territorial boundaries; therefore, states cannot afford the luxury of imposing themselves upon only those who have (or would have) consented. One might suggest that political coercion is legitimate because it produces benefits (and, more importantly, produces benefits for the citizens), but the institution of slavery also produces benefits (and, insofar as slave owners provide food, shelter, and clothing for their slaves, slavery also benefits the slaves themselves). Moreover, one cannot object to slavery on the grounds that it does not provide a *net* benefit to slaves for two reasons. First, it is implausible to suppose that absolutely everyone is better off because of the state's presence (think, for instance, of the rugged individualist who would prefer to take her chances in the state of nature), and thus one could not justify the state's coercion in terms of the net benefits to all those

---

2 Perhaps the most celebrated comparison between political coercion and slavery is Robert Nozick's "Tale of the Slave" in *Anarchy, State, and Utopia* (New York: Basic Books, 1974), 290–2.

3 See A. John Simmons, *Moral Principles and Political Obligation* (Princeton, NJ: Princeton University Press, 1979), especially Chapters III and IV on the absence of consent.

coerced. Second, even if everyone benefited from political coercion, it would be objectionably paternalistic to suppose that
this alone justifies the state's imposition because each of us has
a right to choose whether and precisely how we would like to
be benefited. (An investment company could not justify taking
control of my life savings without my permission merely on the
grounds that its money management would benefit me, for instance.) Finally, it will not suffice to point out that political subjects are generally *happy* to be citizens or that compatriots typically *identify with* one another because not all citizens are happy
to be coerced or identify with their compatriots. What is more,
even if all citizens were either happy to be coerced or identified with one another, it is not clear why this would justify the
coercion; certainly slavery would not be justified even if one's
slaves were happy with the arrangement or identified with one
another.

Thus, when one pauses to look closely at the comparison between slavery and political imposition, one sees that it is surprisingly difficult to distinguish between the two. The key shared
element is *nonconsensual coercion*. This feature that makes slavery
impermissible is also utilized by all governments and thus places
the burden upon any of us who are reluctant to label all political states unjust. Thus, the analogy between slavery and political
coercion appears not only apt, it is helpful insofar as it motivates
the central and most important question of political theory: Why
not be an anarchist?

A Defense of Statism

I am not an anarchist because I believe political states provide vitally important benefits that could not be secured in their absence,
and they supply these benefits without requiring their subjects
to make unreasonable sacrifices. This defense of statism openly
depends upon the truth of three claims: (1) political states supply crucial benefits, (2) these benefits would be unavailable in
the absence of political states, and (3) states can render their
services without imposing unreasonable costs upon those they

coerce.[4] Let me quickly explain why I think each of these premises is plausible.

Perhaps the best way to get a sense of the benefits of political society is to imagine what life would be like if your state were to go completely out of existence. Unless one lives in a very close-knit, face-to-face community where everyone knows each other and is invested in the group as a whole (which almost none of us does), it seems unrealistic to think that life without a political state would be anything but a horribly chaotic and perilous environment where one would lack the security necessary to pursue meaningful projects and relationships. In other words, for the vast majority of us, it would be virtually impossible to live a rewarding life.

Let me stress that in positing this gloomy picture, I do not mean to suggest that all humans would be revealed to be inherently evil; rather, I believe that even well-meaning, rational people would end up in a horrible environment if there were no state. I think that unless the state is present to establish, enforce, and adjudicate a clear and uniform set of rules that everyone must follow, trouble would ensue. The problem is not that everyone would seek to violate the moral rights of others simply because they knew that they were unlikely to be punished (though some undoubtedly would); it is that conflicts would inevitably arise even among morally good people who genuinely prefer a stable and just peace.

Consider briefly just three things that social contract theorists have traditionally cited as unavoidable sources of chaos. First, in the absence of a state there would be no definitive body to establish a salient set of rules; as a consequence, conflicts would abound even among well-meaning people who sincerely disagree over what justice requires. The point here is that, even if one supposes that moral rights exist and are often generally recognizable and recognized by the vast majority of us, devils lurk in the details. Consider, for instance, property rights. Let us

4 I understand "statism" to be merely the denial of anarchism. Thus, all statists believe that political states *can* be justified, and many believe that (at least some) existing states *are* in fact legitimate. The defense of statism I offer here draws upon ideas I introduced in "Liberalism, Samaritanism and Political Legitimacy," *Philosophy & Public Affairs* 25 (1996): 211–37.

assume that everyone agrees that each of us is morally entitled to the fruits of her labor. Even if we all agreed to this general directive and conscientiously sought to respect it, there would be plenty of room for conflict. Problems would inevitably emerge because, although it would presumably be relatively clear that I have a right to the fish I catch in the ocean, very few of modern life's possessions are acquired in such a simple fashion. Our elaborate and sophisticated system of commerce would be impossible without an equally elaborate and sophisticated system of rules to govern property, and such a detailed set of rules is underdetermined by the vague pronouncement that each person has a moral claim to the fruit of her labor. And because people typically care passionately about who gets to keep what property (especially when both parties sincerely believe themselves to be in the right), there is every reason to suppose that these conflicts will often be intractable and not infrequently lead to violence.

Second and more obviously, even if we assume that most people are well-intentioned folks who would never purposely violate the moral rights of others, it is clearly implausible to suppose that *everyone* would be so disposed. Think of it this way: if there is already a nonnegligible number of us who regularly violate the clear rights of others despite the imposing presence of an enormous punitive system designed to apprehend and punish criminals, it seems unrealistic to assume that there would not be considerably more criminal activity if that system were dismantled. (Indeed, it does not require great imagination to appreciate this point; one need only reflect upon what has happened in virtually all cases in which natural or social causes have even temporarily disabled those authorities responsible for enforcing the criminal law.) Moreover, notice that these relatively few criminally oriented people are likely to be a corrupting influence on many of those who would otherwise be inclined to play by the rules. It is not just that borderline people will be more likely to succumb to temptation when they see others routinely getting away with taking from others (though this effect should not be minimized). The more dangerous problem is how the initial victims will react when they realize their relative impotence either to catch and punish those who have wronged them or to ensure that they are not victimized again in the future. It does not seem unreasonable to think that these victims might be more inclined to violate the rights of others (in a misguided attempt to restore themselves to the level to which they consider themselves entitled) and to spend less time and energy on productive projects (the fruits of which are vulnerable to being stolen) and more time on defensive (if not preemptive) efforts designed to retain what is most precious. In fact, one need not have been a victim oneself to recognize the rationality of adopting this defensive strategy; anyone who comprehends the incentives of life without an effective system of criminal law can appreciate the folly of working to acquire portable goods and the wisdom of striving instead to limit one's vulnerability to others. Of course, as people generally produce fewer and fewer new goods, this will increase the temptation to steal those already in circulation, and thus interpersonal relations will continue to deteriorate as each person becomes increasingly fearful of the threat posed by others. In the end, then, it is clear that even if most of us are antecedently disinclined to mistreat others, the absence of an effective system of criminal punishment would create dangerous incentives for those few who do not respect moral rights, which in turn would set in motion a number of other, mutually reinforcing trends whose cumulative effects would be dramatic.

Third and finally, let us suppose that a victim does apprehend someone whom she is convinced has violated her rights. In the absence of a legal system, it now falls upon the victim and her allies to exact restitution and/or mete out punitive justice. And when the punishment is imposed by the victim herself rather than by an impartial third party, three types of complications are prone to arise: (1) the victim may punish an innocent person; (2) the victim may overpunish the wrongdoer; and (3) even if the victim punishes the criminal in accordance with her guilt, the criminal might sincerely believe that she has been either wrongly punished or overpunished.

Regarding (1), victims are more liable to punish innocent people whom they mistake as wrongdoers because they are doubly

biased: Not only might their affections/aversions give them a prej-
udiced sense of who is guilty and innocent, their personal stake
in revenge would understandably lead them (however uncon-
sciously) to reduce the burden of proof for conviction. (Whereas
a legal system might be designed to ensure that ten guilty people are let go before one innocent person is wrongly convicted, it
seems wildly implausible to suppose that a victim seeking personally to impose a punishment on the person she believes violated
her rights would effectively operate according to anything like
that directive.) Impartial judges and jurors, on the other hand, are
not as personally invested in the case. Their paramount concern
is simply to see that justice is served, and as a result they are much
less likely to convict the innocent. Analogous reasoning applies
to (2): Because the victim is so concerned to be avenged/restored,
she may be inclined to demand too much compensation and/or
impose too stiff a penalty. Finally, concerning (3), it is important to note that even if, as an objective matter, the criminal is
not subjected to excessive punishment, she is likely genuinely to
believe that she has been treated unfairly. This belief could em-
anate from any of three sources: First, it would not be surprising
for a wrongdoer to incorrectly but sincerely believe that she has
not violated the victim's moral rights (this is especially likely in
an anarchic environment where there is no authoritative body
to establish and promulgate an undisputed code of criminal law).
Second, the same personal bias that often leads the victim to believe that the criminal deserves a harsher penalty would lead
the wrongdoer to favor her own perspective, and thus sincerely
to believe that she deserves a more lenient punishment. Third,
given that the punishment meted out by the victim herself appears more personal and less authoritative, the person punished
is all the more likely to regard the punishment as an excessive
personal indulgence rather than as an appropriate execution of
justice.

Now, (1)–(3) are all significant because each one is likely to
inspire retaliation. To appreciate the importance of this point,
consider how Jennifer and her friends and family would likely
react if Jane imposed punishment X upon Jennifer for crime Y,

and either (1) Jennifer is in fact innocent of crime Y, (2) punishment X is excessive for crime Y, or (3) for whatever reason, Jennifer and her allies sincerely believe that punishment X is excessive for crime Y. In each case, Jennifer and her supporters would be convinced that Jane has wrongly harmed Jennifer and thus are likely to set out to exact retribution for what they regard as Jane's wrongful or excessive punishment. The problem, of course, is that Jane and her allies will not believe that the initial punishment violated Jennifer's rights, and thus they will regard any attempt to punish Jane as a mere criminal attack. As a consequence, the longer Jane's allies are able to protect her from punishment, the more Jennifer and her supporters will be likely to resort to extreme measures to exact some sort of revenge. If Jennifer and her allies are able swiftly to impose a punishment, on the other hand, then we should expect Jane and her friends and family to be especially incensed that Jennifer has (at least from Jane's perspective) now violated Jane's rights for a second time. In short, if the state were to disappear and criminal punishment were then left up to those sufficiently interested in the particular crimes to take matters into their own hands, it is hard to see how things would not soon deteriorate into a bloody mess.

To recapitulate, in the absence of a political state, one should expect three especially glaring problems to emerge. Without an authoritative legislative body to establish a definitive set of rules that everyone must follow, there will be conflicts even among well-intentioned people who genuinely seek to treat each other according to the demands of morality. Without an effective executive body to ensure that a reasonable percentage of rule breakers are caught and punished, those disinclined to respect the moral rights of others will not be sufficiently deterred and, ultimately, everyone's incentives to pursue productive projects and meaningful relationships will diminish markedly. Finally, without a standing judicial body to impartially adjudicate conflicts and assign criminal punishments, attempts to exact revenge and mete out justice will lead to increasingly bloody conflicts. Moreover, it is important to recognize that the cumulative effect of these three factors is more than additive; these elements will combine to create a vicious cycle in which each consideration presents an aggravating factor that exacerbates the others.

It is hard to exaggerate how horrible life would be in the absence of political security, but one theorist who has been accused of doing so is Thomas Hobbes. He famously describes life without political order (often referred to as the "state of nature") as follows:

> Hereby it is manifest, that during the time men live without a common Power to keep them all in awe, they are in that condition which is called Warre; and such a warre, as is of every man, against every man. . . . Whatsoever therefore is consequent to a time of Warre, where every man is Enemy to every man; the same is consequent to the time, wherein men live without other security, than what their own strength, and their own invention shall furnish them withall. In such condition, there is no place for Industry; because the fruit thereof is uncertain: and consequently no Culture of the Earth; no Navigation, nor use of the commodities that may be imported by Sea; no commodious Building; no Instruments of moving, and removing such things as require much force; no Knowledge of the face of the Earth; no account of Time; no Arts; no Letters; no Society; and which is worst of all, continuall feare, and danger of violent death; And the life of man, solitary, poore, nasty, brutish, and short.[5]

Certainly there is reason to quibble with various details of Hobbes's description of the state of nature as well as his elaborate argument in support of that description, but it strikes me as difficult to deny the general picture. Put plainly, for the vast majority of us, life without political order would be a horribly perilous environment.

Part of the explanation for why I am not an anarchist, then, is that states perform incredibly important legislative, executive, and judicial functions. Given that states are nonconsensually coercive, however, it is not enough to point out that states perform these beneficial functions. Clearly, we would prefer to have these

---

5 Thomas Hobbes, *Leviathan*, Part I, Chapter 13, paragraphs 8 and 9.

functions performed via some noncoercive means, so an adequate defense of statism must also demonstrate that these benefits could not be secured in the absence of political order. It is here that anarchists often press their case, arguing that statists are too quick to conclude that life would necessarily be unbearable in the absence of political order. One might think that life in the state of nature would be fine if one had a great deal of confidence in human nature or the motivational force of morality, but one need not have such utopian inclinations to be an anarchist. More often, anarchists challenge the necessity of states in one of two standard ways: Some insist that political coercion is not necessary in close-knit communities, and others maintain that states are never necessary because private companies could perform the functions in question. Consider each of these views in turn.

The Anarchist's Rejoinder

Anarchists who emphasize the strength of communities argue that the three types of problems I have outlined might very well arise in many cases, but they would be unlikely to occur in healthy communities, especially small-scale, close-knit groups in which virtually everyone personally knows everyone else. The central idea here is that when the bonds between individuals are sufficiently robust, we need not fear the chaos about which statists warn us because (1) the community would have the resources both to establish and to educate all of its members about a workable set of rules; (2) the fellow feeling among community members would make people disinclined to mistreat one another; and, (3) because everyone would identify so closely with everyone else and the community as a whole, group members would not only happily protect each other's rights, they would work together to apprehend and punish anyone who flouted the community's rules.

Although I find this optimistic view of communal life attractive, I am skeptical that contemporary communities could function in anything like this fashion, except in the most rare and abnormal circumstances. In particular, while many anarchists of this persuasion suggest that contemporary communities would undoubtedly be more robust were it not for the corrupting influence of the modern bureaucratic state, I suspect that the opposite is true. My own view is that many contemporary communities are able to flourish to the extent that they do only because they are sheltered by stable political states that not only buttress the communities' norms (by threatening to punish those community members who violate the rights of others) but also deter outsiders from wrongly interfering with the community's self-determination. As a consequence, I question whether the communal prescription for peace and stability is one that could even in theory be widely effective today.

It is important to notice, though, that even if states have historically played a prominent causal role in the destruction of communal bonds, this would not be enough to vindicate the view in question. This form of anarchism would still be implausible because – whatever is to blame for our current lack of communal ties – the undeniable fact is that virtually all of us not only do not live in sufficiently close-knit communities, we lack the means to cultivate such communities in the foreseeable future. This point is decisive, of course, because it implies that – however different things might have been if history had unfolded according to an alternative script – the vast majority of us do not have the communal resources to restore the order that would be disrupted in the absence of the state's coercive presence, and thus we would in fact be imperiled if our states were to go out of existence. In short, even if communal anarchists are right to be optimistic about the benefits communities might have been able to supply had history unfolded differently, this counterfactual claim gives us no reason to doubt that states are necessary in this actual world.

An alternative defense of anarchism concedes that we need institutions to protect us from perilous vulnerability, but it denies that we need the nonconsensual institutions of a state. According to this view, any function that a government might perform a private company could perform better. Thus, there is no reason that one could not hire a protective company to protect one's moral rights better and/or less expensively than states currently do. As a consequence, even though states undeniably supply precious benefits, these same benefits could be supplied in their absence and, therefore, there is no justification for the nonconsensual coercion that invariably attends political states.

I have a great deal of sympathy for this approach because I believe that modern states have indeed ballooned to unjustifiable proportions. In my view, too many of us naively presume that states would not interfere where they do not belong, when in fact states have demonstrated a lamentable tendency to insert themselves into all types of matters where their presence is not only unnecessary but positively harmful. However, despite my conviction that we must guard against states wrongly assigning themselves additional responsibilities, I remain a statist because I continue to believe that no other type of institution could solve the legislative, executive, and judicial problems enumerated previously. States are necessary because hazardous chaos would unavoidably result unless all those in spatial proximity play by the same rules, and there is no way to get everyone to accede to the same set of rules in the absence of a territorially defined state. In other words, I do not think it is a mere accident that states are defined territorially; on the contrary, the class of people any given state coerces must be delineated geographically (as opposed to by, say, religion or eye color) because governments could not perform their requisite functions unless they uniformly coerced everyone within their territorial boundaries. This is because the legislative, executive, and judicial problems outlined previously would prevail as long as people in close proximity did not defer to a single authority and a definitive set of rules. And since people with various eye colors and differing religions live among one another, it would not be feasible to politically sort subjects according to either of these (or any other nonterritorial) criteria. This observation helps us see why private companies are necessarily ill equipped to secure a lasting and just peace. The great appeal of private protection agencies is that, by serving only those clients who freely sign up, they promise to supply the crucial benefits without any nonconsensual coercion. This solution's chief virtue leads to its ultimate downfall, however, because no genuinely voluntary arrangement would garner universal subscription, and thus none would avoid the violent division we seek to avoid. Let me explain.

For a variety of reasons, no private protection agency would win everyone's business. First, a number of individuals would not hire any company simply because they cannot afford to pay for the service. (And, in the absence of a state to pool resources and provide a guaranteed social safety net, there is no telling how large this group might be.) Some among those who could afford the service would prefer to hire no company for the same reason that they eschew the government – they are rugged individualists who would rather take their chances on their own. More importantly, however, we should expect those who would hire a protective agency to spread themselves out among a number of competing firms. Such division is inevitable because, in the absence of a state to impose a monopolistic supplier, we must assume that individuals would be drawn to a variety of private companies, all of which would compete zealously for customers and the substantial profits at stake.

Given the presence of competing private protection agencies, it takes little imagination to see how peace and stability would be undermined. The central problem, of course, is that each agency would be concerned first and foremost with maximizing profits, and, as such, its prime objective would be to acquire and retain clients. This desire to attract customers would lead firms to concern themselves principally with marketing and client representation, and thus Jane's firm and Jennifer's agency would be liable to conflict in the same ways (and for analogous reasons) that Jane and Jennifer as individuals would have. That is, if one of Jane's moral rights is violated, then the company Jane has hired to protect her from harm would have a financial interest in apprehending and exacting restitution from the wrongdoer. (Or, more accurately, Jane's protective agency would have a financial interest in apprehending someone whom *Jane will be convinced* is the wrongdoer and exacting *what Jane believes* is just restitution.) In other words, Jane's company (like Jane herself) is emphatically *not* an unbiased third party merely working to see that justice is done; it is an interested party, and, as such, it is prone to punish the innocent and overpunish the guilty. Moreover, just as Jennifer was liable incorrectly to see herself as either wrongly punished or overpunished by Jane, Jennifer is apt to see herself as either wrongly punished or overpunished by the company Jane has hired to secure her moral rights. Thus, once Jennifer has been punished, she may very well complain to her own company that her rights have been violated. What is more, the ensuing conflict between Jennifer's company and Jane's agency would be just as intractable as the analogous conflict between Jennifer and Jane would have been because the goal of the employees in Jane's (Jennifer's) agency would not be to secure what is in fact just; it would be to retain Jane's (Jennifer's) business, which they could reasonably expect to do only if they secured what Jane (Jennifer) *believes* is just. Thus, the introduction of private agencies could not eliminate the conflicts that we should expect to arise in the state of nature (and in many ways it may magnify them since these conflicts would occur between larger, more potent groups) because as long as people have a genuinely free choice as to which (if any) agency to hire, there will still be no single party with the authority to definitively establish a common set of rules, to effectively and uniformly enforce these rules, and to impartially adjudicate potential conflicts under these rules. The only way to ensure that everyone will in fact defer to such an ultimate authority is if this authority imposes itself with irresistible force upon everyone within the territorial limits.

If the preceding account is correct, then it is no longer so difficult to distinguish between political coercion and slavery: Both resort to nonconsensual coercion to generate benefits, but only governments produce crucial benefits that could not be supplied in their absence. In light of this morally relevant difference, clearly there is nothing logically inconsistent or otherwise hypocritical about being a statist, on the one hand, and condemning slavery, on the other. However, while noting the nature of the benefits available only in political society points to the logical space for a defense of political coercion, it is not on its own enough to supply this defense. In my view, political coercion is in fact justified only if, unlike slavery, it does not impose unreasonable costs upon those nonconsensually coerced. In other words, if the imposition of a political state were as burdensome to its subjects as slavery typically is to those enslaved, then political coercion would presumably not be justified even if it were necessary to rescue us from the perils of the state of nature. As I will now explain, however, states can be legitimate as long as they perform their requisite functions without imposing too great a burden upon their subjects.

Samaritanism and Voluntarism

To begin, let me acknowledge that modern states demand considerable sacrifices from their subjects. As I emphasized in my initial comparison between slavery and political coercion, states not only coerce their subjects in myriad ways, they tax these subjects in order to amass the force necessary to make their coercion practically irresistible. In other words, states impose a substantial secondary cost (taxes) in order to secure their ability to impose their primary coercion (the creation, enforcement, and adjudication of laws). But even though these primary and secondary costs are unquestionably substantial, the *net* costs of citizenship are not unreasonably great because these net costs consist of these admittedly considerable initial costs *minus* the even greater benefits of political stability.

I say that the benefits of citizenship are greater than the costs because what each of us gains from everyone else's compliance with the state's laws is much more valuable than what we lose by having to obey these laws ourselves. Certainly we would prefer to retain the discretion to act in accordance with our own personal interpretation of what morality requires (and obviously we would rather not pay our taxes), but the cumulative result of everyone enjoying this discretion is the perilous environment explained earlier. Thus, by producing benefits that far outweigh its costs, it is as if the state forced each of its constituents to give up a hundred dollar bill but in return gave back ten twenties.

Presumably it is obvious to most that these benefits far outweigh the admittedly considerable costs, but if you are not yet convinced, consider the following thought experiment. Imagine that a supremely powerful government official approached you with an extraordinary offer: If you are content to continue obeying the law and paying your taxes, then she will keep your current state in place as is; if you would rather be freed from your state's imposition, on the other hand, then she will entirely disband your current state. How would you choose? I concede that there may be some exceptionally optimistic and/or self-reliant people who would genuinely choose for the state to be disbanded, but I have little doubt that virtually every informed person would choose to continue obeying the laws and paying her taxes. As much as we might resent the burdens of citizenship, I suspect that almost all of us would admit that the benefits of political society far outweigh the costs.

Let me stress, however, that I highlight the profound benefits of living in political society only to support my assertion that the net costs of citizenship are not unreasonably onerous; I am emphatically *not* suggesting that states are justified in coercing their constituents because this coercion ultimately benefits each of them.[6] I reject this latter approach for two reasons. First, as I have acknowledged throughout, there may be a few subjects (robust individualists, for instance, who place an extraordinary premium on self-reliance) who very well might be better off in a state of nature. And, if so, then a straightforward appeal to the benefits for each citizen would not suffice to justify the state's coercion of everyone. Second and more important, I object to the paternalism implicit in any account that justifies nonconsensual coercion in terms of potential benefits to the coercee. In my view, each competent adult enjoys a privileged position of moral dominion over her own self-regarding affairs, and this dominion entails that each of us must be allowed to choose which benefits

---

6 For this reason it would be wrong to think, as some critics have suggested, that my reference to the profound benefits of political society necessarily renders my account paternalistic. See, for example, George Klosko, "Samaritanism and Political Obligation: A Response to Christopher Wellman's 'Liberal Theory of Political Obligation'," *Ethics* 113 (2003): 835–40.

to pursue. As a result, one may not permissibly coerce another, even if one knows that doing so will benefit the coercee. As I mentioned earlier, just as my investment broker may not put a gun to my head and insist that I invest my money in a particular beneficial fashion, my state cannot justify its coercion of me in terms of how this coercion benefits me.

The preceding does not render the benefits of political society beside the point, however; these crucial benefits remain relevant because they substantiate my claim that political coercion is not unreasonably costly. This is important because I want to insist that a state is justified in nonconsensually coercing *me* (even if I am not benefited and/or would genuinely prefer to take my chances in the state of nature) because the state's uniform coercion over all those within its territorial borders is the only way for it rescue *any of us* from the perils of the state of nature. My account of political legitimacy is nonpaternalistic, then, because it insists that my state may justifiably coerce *me* only because this coercion is a necessary and not unreasonably burdensome means of securing crucial benefits for *others*. To emphasize: According to the defense of statism I advocate here, my state is ultimately permitted to coerce me only because this coercion is both (1) necessary to secure vitally important benefits for my compatriots and (2) not unreasonably costly to myself. Thus, I openly concede that political coercion is doubly like slavery insofar as the coercion is both nonconsensual and – at least in part – designed to benefit others. I insist that political states can nonetheless be justified, however, because the beneficial functions they perform are essential to living a minimally rewarding life, and states can perform these functions without imposing excessive costs on their citizens. In short, although political coercion admittedly shares crucial features with slavery, it is importantly distinct not only because slavery is not necessary to provide others with vitally important benefits, but also because slavery imposes unacceptable costs upon those enslaved.

At this point, a critic might object that I have succeeded only in showing that political coercion is a milder type of slavery. My arguments may demonstrate that political coercion is less objectionable than the more traditional chattel slavery, but that it remains impermissible precisely because of the moral dominion I have just cited to explain the wrongness of paternalism. In other words, one might protest that even if it is true that others would be horribly imperiled unless I were coerced, this does not license coercing me without my permission as long as I am not personally responsible for their impending peril. This objection depends upon a particularly austere form of voluntarism, and while I acknowledge that some voluntarist accounts of morality can be attractive, no plausible version of voluntarism would exclude the moral premises necessary for the defense of statism offered here.

In its most extreme form, voluntarism is the view that one is morally bound in no ways that one has not voluntarily accepted. Virtually no one endorses voluntarism in this unqualified guise, however, because it has obviously unpalatable implications, such as that Albert does no wrong in killing Bob unless Albert has voluntarily agreed not to do so. A less severe voluntarism that applies only to our positive obligations is more popular, however.[7] According to this modified view, each of us has a natural (i.e., nonvoluntary) duty not to harm others, but no one can have a positive duty to benefit others unless she has voluntarily accepted this duty. The idea motivating this theory is the intuitively compelling notion that each of us should be free to be the authors of our own lives, and this freedom entails that others cannot unilaterally foist (positive) moral obligations upon us. Or (put in terms of the moral dominion I invoked previously), each of us enjoys a privileged position of moral dominion over her self-regarding affairs, and since any behavior that does not wrongly harm others is self-regarding, we are entitled to be free from coercion as long as we are not wrongly harming others.

Although this second, more limited version of voluntarism comes much closer to the truth, it remains too ambitious. In particular, it is implausible to insist that we occupy a position of absolute moral dominion over our self-regarding affairs *no matter*

---

7 "Positive" duties require us to assist others; they are to be contrasted with "negative" duties, which require merely that we not harm or interfere with others.

how dire the circumstances of others may be. Surely there are extreme circumstances in which it would be permissible to encroach upon what would ordinarily be a person's position of moral dominion. Imagine, for instance, that Amy has a seizure, desperately needs medical attention, and can be saved only if Beth immediately commandeers Cathy's car and drives Amy to the nearest hospital. Would it be permissible for Beth to take Cathy's car, or would it be wrong even in these extreme circumstances for Beth to use Cathy's property without the latter's permission? Most would agree that Beth may permissibly take Cathy's car. Certainly Beth should return it as promptly as possible (and perhaps Beth or Amy should offer Cathy some type of compensation for having taken Cathy's property without her permission), but it strikes me that the extreme circumstances justify Beth's acting in a manner that ordinarily would be impermissible. That is, whereas Cathy's property right in her car would ordinarily make Beth's action impermissible, the fact that Amy's life hangs in the balance gives Beth's mission an urgency that outweighs Cathy's normally decisive dominion over her self-regarding affairs.

Returning to voluntarism, it is important to notice that even the modified version of voluntarism we are now considering would *not* permit Beth to take Cathy's car because, given that Cathy was in no way responsible for Amy's seizure, Cathy would continue to enjoy an absolute position of dominion over her car. In light of this, clearly voluntarism must be further qualified so as to leave room for our dominion to be permissibly encroached on in sufficiently dire circumstances. Such an amendment does not constitute abandoning voluntarism; it merely involves recognizing that voluntarism applies to an extensive but duly limited sphere. Indeed, John Simmons, one of the most impressive and prominent defenders of *political* voluntarism, would apparently have no qualms with such a move. As he puts it: "just as obligations sometimes ought not to be discharged, so rights may sometimes be legitimately infringed. I do not act wrongly in taking your car without permission (and so violating your property rights) or failing to deliver the product I sold you (violating your contractual rights), if these acts and omissions are necessary to save someone from great and unmerited harm. Our rights may sometimes be infringed in the performance of important duties or to prevent extremely unhappy occurrences."[8] Thus, while some might argue that voluntarism requires further qualification, clearly voluntarists must at least acknowledge that one's privileged position of dominion allows one neither to wrongly harm others nor to fail to benefit others when they are sufficiently imperiled and one can help them at no unreasonable cost to oneself. Once voluntarism has been qualified to this minimal extent, however, it is entirely compatible with the account of political legitimacy I have outlined.

This less austere version of voluntarism leaves ample room for statism because a state's nonconsensual coercion of its citizens is morally analogous to Beth's nonconsensual borrowing of Cathy's car insofar as each is necessary "to prevent extremely unhappy occurrences." Just as it would ordinarily be impermissible for Beth to take Cathy's car without the latter's permission, it is typically unjustified to nonconsensually coerce someone. Just as Beth's unauthorized use of Cathy's car is made permissible only because this course of action is the only way to rescue Amy from her extreme peril, a state's coercion of its constituents is justified only because this imposition is the only way to rescue any of them from the perilous chaos that would otherwise prevail. Just as Beth would not be permitted to take a course of action dramatically more costly to Cathy (like chopping off one of Cathy's arms) *even if this were the only way to save Amy's life*, the state would not be justified in coercing its citizens if this coercion were unreasonably costly (as it would be if the costs of citizenship – like slavery – were dramatically more substantial than the benefits) *even if this were*

---

8 A. John Simmons, *Justification and Legitimacy* (Cambridge: Cambridge University Press, 2001), 60–1. It is important to note that, although Simmons is a celebrated advocate of *political* voluntarism, he has never defended *moral* voluntarism in any of the guises I am considering here. It is therefore open to him to grant my qualifications of moral voluntarism and yet continue to defend an unqualified version of political voluntarism. Such a position might strike some as awkward, however. At the very least, a political voluntarist who granted the existence of nonvoluntary (positive) moral duties would seem to owe us an explanation for why no *political* duty could be nonvoluntary. As far as I know, Simmons has not yet offered such an explanation.

the only way to rescue everyone from the state of nature. In sum, just as Beth's nonconsensual taking of Cathy's car is permissible only because this course of action is both (1) necessary to save Amy and (2) not an unreasonable imposition upon Cathy, a legitimate state's nonconsensual coercion of all those within its territorial limits is justified only because it is both (1) necessary to save everyone in that territory from the perils of a lawless environment and (2) not an unreasonable imposition upon those coerced.

Before moving on, it is worth explicitly acknowledging each of the various assumptions required for my defense of statism. The twin descriptive premises, of course, are simply that (1) states secure vital benefits that (2) could not be secured by any other, noncoercive means. It is important to notice, however, that there is a third premise implicit in my claim that states can perform these functions without imposing any *unreasonable* burdens upon their constituents. Insofar as the plausibility of this claim depends in part upon the great benefits of political society, this premise might appear wholly descriptive, but it also contains a moral claim. It includes an ineliminably moral element because it asserts that, given the costs and benefits of political coercion, no constituent may righteously object to this coercion, and, as such, it involves the moral claim that one's normally decisive position of moral dominion can be overridden by particularly urgent, and therefore morally preemptory, concerns.

I have said a good bit in defense of the twin descriptive premises presented previously, so let me briefly suggest why this moral premise – which I call "samaritanism" – is merely a standard component of commonsense morality. First, notice that legal institutions typically allow a "necessity" defense for those who break a law in order prevent some more dire consequence. Beth would likely not be criminally punished for exceeding the legal speed limit en route to the hospital, for instance, as long as she could establish that she did so only to save Amy's life. Moreover, it is important to appreciate that the legal defense of necessity was created in order to accommodate our ordinary moral thinking on these matters. Voluntarists are certainly right to insist that we must largely be left free to determine the moral content of our own lives, but one can accept the moral significance of samaritanism without unduly undermining this voluntarist vision. To invoke a standard example, for instance, notice that virtually no one would insist that a lounger by a pool has no duty to save a drowning child from the pool unless she has freely agreed to do so. On the contrary, ordinary moral thinking dictates that our legitimate interest in pursuing our own self-regarding projects is outweighed in this instance by the twin facts that someone else is in dire need and that one can rescue her at minimal cost to oneself. Thus, this duty to perform easy rescues in particular, and samaritanism in general, clearly involves a moral claim, but it is a commonly accepted and entirely defensible one.

Having acknowledged my moral premise of samaritanism, I am now in a position to complete my defense of statism. I am not an anarchist, even though I recognize that political coercion bears a striking resemblance to slavery, because political states are the only thing capable of rescuing us from the state of nature, and they are able to perform the functions that rescue us from this peril without imposing unacceptable costs upon anyone. If I became convinced that (1) states did not perform these vitally important functions, (2) the crucial benefits could be secured by some other, less coercive means, or (3) political coercion was unreasonably costly, then I would indeed be an anarchist. To conclude in terms of the bumper sticker mentioned at the beginning of this chapter, I am ultimately a statist because I believe there are straightforward and morally relevant grounds on which to distinguish between political coercion and slavery.

Before concluding this chapter, I should acknowledge that a critic might invoke the distinction between *political* and *philosophical* anarchism and argue that my arguments at most undermine the former. John Horton explains the distinction between these two versions of anarchism:

> Political anarchists are more inclined to view the state as an evil institution which must be destroyed if human beings are to flourish. On their view, not merely do people have no political obligation to their state, they should actively oppose its existence. Philosophical anarchists on the other hand, while

denying that states have any distinctive moral authority, do not necessarily conclude from this that the state should be abolished. The political implications of philosophical anarchism are much more open-ended. In short, political anarchists are principally exercised by the practical effects of the state, especially its allegedly socially destructive consequences, while philosophical anarchists are more narrowly identified by their denying to the state any claim to moral authority.[9]

As things stand, this objection is right on target: I have yet to say anything about a citizen's duty to obey the laws of her state, so even if the preceding defense of statism is thoroughly convincing, it defeats only political anarchism, not philosophical anarchism. My case against philosophical anarchism will not be complete until the next chapter, when I draw upon my defense of statism to develop a samaritan account of our duty to obey the law. Before closing this chapter, however, I would like briefly to suggest why there are reasons to suspect that one cannot be a philosophical anarchist without also being a political anarchist. If so, then philosophical anarchism will have much more radical implications than its adherents typically acknowledge.

Aware that political anarchism is so controversial, philosophical anarchists often take great pains to distance their position from the extreme view that we should all join in the fight to dismantle existing governments. John Simmons, the most sophisticated and celebrated philosophical anarchist, puts it as follows:

> What is distinctive about philosophical anarchism is that its judgment of state illegitimacy ... does not translate into any immediate requirement of opposition to illegitimate states. This is what leads many to contrast philosophical anarchism to political anarchism.
>
> Philosophical anarchists hold that there may be good reasons not to oppose or disrupt at least some kinds of illegitimate states, reasons that outweigh any right or obligation of opposition. The practical stance with respect to the state, the philosophical anarchist maintains, should be one of careful consideration and

9 John Horton, *Political Obligation* (Atlantic Highlands, NJ: Humanities Press, 1992), 114.

thoughtful weighing of all of the reasons that bear on action in a particular set of political circumstances. The illegitimacy of a state (and the absence of binding political obligations that it entails) is just one moral factor among many bearing on how persons in that state should (or are permitted to) act. Even illegitimate states, for instance, may have virtues, unaffected by the defects that undermine their legitimacy, that are relevant considerations in determining how we ought to act with respect to those states, and the refusal to do what the law requires is, at least in most (even illegitimate) states, often wrong on independent moral grounds (i.e., the conduct would be wrong even were it not legally forbidden). So there may be a variety of sound moral reasons not to oppose or not to act contrary to the laws of even some illegitimate states.[10]

As a strictly logical matter, these philosophical anarchists are undoubtedly correct: There is logical space to affirm a state's moral liberty right to coerce its constituents and to deny its moral claim right to obedience.[11] In other words, it might be that political subjects have no moral duty to obey the commands of their state *even though the state has a moral right to nonconsensually impose itself upon all those within its territory.* As a practical matter, however, I think it is very difficult simultaneously to endorse philosophical anarchism without also committing oneself to political anarchism. Let me quickly explain the source of this difficulty, first in terms of Simmons's work and then in terms of the more general analogy between slavery and taxation with which this chapter began.

In defending philosophical anarchism, Simmons often compares political states to private companies in order to illustrate that, even if a particular state is internally just, is marvelously efficient, and/or does any number of good deeds, these facts do not in themselves obligate us to support it any more than we would be obligated to support any given company that happens to be

10 Simmons, *Justification and Legitimacy*, 109.
11 I should stress that Simmons has never, to my knowledge, sought to defend a state's general liberty right to coerce its constituents. At most, he has claimed that states may be *in particular cases* morally justified in coercing, as may anyone. As I will argue, it is the generally coercive nature of states that should be worrisome to a political voluntarist like Simmons.

just, efficient, or charitably engaged in good acts. As Simmons puts it: "The fact that a state or a business has virtues appropriate to it cannot, by itself, argue for its having special rights over me or for my owing it special obligations, nor, of course, do these special rights and obligations, where they exist, necessarily over-ride moral duties to oppose a vicious state. Only if the state also has special relations to me will special rights or obligations of that sort follow."[12] The conclusion to which Simmons invites us is that a state is just like a company, and, as a result, while there may be times when we have moral reasons to support a state in its production of benefits, there is no general obligation to obey all of its legal commands. I fear that this analogy between a state and a company may be misleading, however, because unlike a typical company, states depend for their existence upon nonconsensually coercing all those living within their territorial borders. And since Simmons's political voluntarism should lead him to regard such coercion as unjustified, presumably he should think that everyone has moral reasons to resist the state in order to free others from this nonvoluntary coercion (just as we would have reason to resist a company that nonconsensually coerced its "clients"). Certainly Simmons would be right to protest that his view does not commit him to the position that we have an *absolute* duty to *always* resist the state (as he puts it, "The practical stance with respect to the state ... should be one of careful consideration and thoughtful weighing of all the reasons that bear on action in a particular set of political circumstances"[13]), but any thoughtful political anarchist would agree with this. The crucial point is that if a state is nonconsensually coercive despite having no special rights over us, then it seems appropriate to conclude that, other things being equal, we have moral reasons to actively resist the state. And this last conclusion, of course, is *political* – not merely *philosophical* – anarchism. In short, Simmons's view may be more radical than he admits because his defense of philosophical anarchism appears to lead not only to the claim that we have no

---

12 Simmons, *Justification and Legitimacy*, p. 112.
13 Ibid., 109.

general obligation to support the state but also to the conclusion that we should all work to overthrow the state.

To appreciate that this difficulty does not arise merely from Simmons's analogy between political states and private companies, notice that it can equally well be explained in terms of the comparison between taxation and slavery with which this chapter began. Bumper stickers that proclaim "Taxation is slavery!" are motivationally efficacious because everyone appreciates that if political coercion were really morally tantamount to slavery, then we would be no more obligated to obey the laws of our state than a slave would be morally bound to obey her master's commands. (And this, of course, is precisely why I went to such lengths to distinguish between the two.) But notice: If my arguments to this point have been inadequate and political coercion were really analogous to slavery, then it would not merely follow that we have no obligation to obey the law; in addition, we should conclude that, just as we all would have moral reasons to work to eliminate the injustice of slavery, each of us ought to take to the streets to end the oppression of political coercion. Think of it in these terms: When it comes to slavery, it would be highly implausible to adopt a stance of "philosophical abolitionism," insisting that slaves have no moral obligation to obey their masters but denying that slavery is necessarily impermissible. No one would endorse such a muted form of abolitionism because the same feature of slavery that explains why slaves are not obligated to obey their masters (i.e., nonconsensual coercion) equally explains why it is impermissible to enslave others. Thus, it seems at the very least awkward to support the analogous position regarding political states – philosophical anarchism – which insists that citizens have no moral obligation to obey the law but denies that there is anything morally problematic about imposing this law in the first place.

To reiterate what might be dubbed the "bricks and bottles" objection: As much as philosophical anarchists might strive to divorce themselves from the awkward position that we should be in the streets throwing bricks and bottles in an attempt to overthrow the state, there is reason to suspect that any argument that calls into question our duty to obey the law can equally be applied, *mutatis mutandis*, to the state's right to exist. If so, then philosophical anarchists bear more of an argumentative burden than they typically let on. Not only must they demonstrate why no existing explanation of our duty to obey the law suffices, it is incumbent upon them to show why their arguments do not also lead to the less palatable conclusion that we should take to the streets to dismantle all existing states.

2   Doing One's Fair Share

EVEN if the considerations offered in the preceding chapter conclusively defeat political anarchism, they are not by themselves sufficient to refute *philosophical* anarchism because they do not explain why one has a duty to obey the law.[1] A citizen's political responsibilities have yet to be established because the focus to this point has been exclusively upon the permissibility of a state's coercing its constituents, not the political duties of those coerced. I am hopeful that we can develop an adequate account of our duty to obey the law, however, by building upon the defense of statism offered earlier. In particular, I think that just as samaritanism is crucial to justifying the state's coercion, it is the key to explaining our political duties.[2]

Samaritan Duties and Fairness

The first thing to notice is that the peril of others can explain not only why one may permissibly be coerced, it can also explain why

---

1 For the purposes of this essay, I draw no distinction between "duties" and "obligations." What is more, unless I specify otherwise, I understand all duties to be perfect and enforceable. In other words, I will not use the term "duty" in cases that might be thought of either as "imperfect" duties or as matters of virtue. (In these cases, I shall most often speak of an agent as merely having "moral reasons" to do something.)
2 The account of our duty to obey the law I defend later draws upon my arguments in "Toward a Liberal Theory of Political Obligation," *Ethics* 111 (2001): 735–59, and "Political Obligation and the Particularity Requirement," *Legal Theory* 10 (2004): 97–115.

one is obligated to assist those who are imperiled. (Indeed, if any-thing, it is more common and less controversial to posit samaritan duties than to defend the existence of a samaritan right to coerce.) Thus, just as I invoked samaritanism to explain why Beth may permissibly commandeer Cathy's car if it is the only way to get Amy to the hospital in time to save her life, samaritanism can help explain why Beth has a duty to take Amy to the hospital and/or why Cathy has a duty to loan her car to the cause. The central idea here should be apparent in light of our earlier dis-cussion of the room any plausible version of voluntarism must leave for samaritanism: Although voluntarists are no doubt cor-rect that we should be largely free to determine the content of our special moral responsibilities, moral duties may in fact be unilat-erally foisted upon us in extreme circumstances, when others are sufficiently imperiled and we can help them at no unreasonable cost to ourselves. This is why virtually no one denies that one would have a moral duty to wade into a shallow pond to save a drowning baby, for instance, even if this rescue requires one to get one's shoes and trousers wet.

Once samaritan duties are acknowledged, it does not take much imagination to see how we can draw upon the forego-ing defense of statism to explain our duty to obey the law. If the peril that others would endure in the state of nature is suffi-ciently grave to justify coercing me without my consent, then it stands to reason that this very same peril could ground my duty to perform an easy rescue. Thus, given that states rescue us all from the perilous circumstances that would inevitably prevail in their absence, and because states rely upon the compliance of their constituents to perform their political functions, it seems to follow that each of us has a samaritan duty to obey the law. In other words, just as Amy's medical peril can render Beth duty bound to rush Amy to the hospital, the potential peril of my compatriots can obligate me to obey the laws of my state. The vehicle required to save Amy is Cathy's car, and the vehicle re-quired to save my compatriots is our state; but Beth's *duty* is to drive this car, and my *duty* is to obey the legal commands of my state.

Thus, our first formulation of the samaritan account is that each of us has a duty to obey the law because this obedience rescues our compatriots from the perils of the state of nature. I specify that this is a "first formulation" because, in order for obedience to the law to qualify as a samaritan duty, it must be both (1) not unreasonably costly and (2) in fact necessary to rescue others from peril. And, as I shall now explain, the cost condition does not present insuperable problems, but the necessity condition does require us to supplement and refine our account.

First, notice that a citizen's obedience to the law could qualify as an "easy" rescue even though states sometimes make considerable demands upon their constituents. As noted earlier, it is plausible to construe obedience to the state's laws as not unreasonably costly because one must consider the great benefits along with the admittedly substantial costs of citizenship. Once these benefits are subtracted from the costs, there is nothing awkward about labeling the *net* costs as not unreasonable, and thus there is nothing incoherent about classifying obedience to the law as an easy rescue.

Problems emerge with the necessity condition, however, because it appears that my compliance with the state's legal commands is not in fact necessary to save others from the perils of the state of nature. To appreciate the significance of this fact, recall that samaritanism becomes morally operative only when a particular course is essential to save the imperiled person. Thus, Beth would not be morally entitled to commandeer Cathy's car unless this course of action was in fact necessary to get Amy to the hospital in time. (If Beth could just as quickly and easily get Amy there in a taxi, for instance, then Beth would have no right to take Cathy's car.) Similarly, I went to such lengths in the preceding chapter to establish that a tolerable level of order could not be achieved in the absence of territorially defined states because political coercion would not be justified unless it were indeed necessary to eliminate the perilous chaos of life in a state of nature. (If private companies could secure a just peace without nonconsensually coercing anyone, for instance, then I would reject statism.) This raises difficulties for the straightforward samaritan account of our duty to obey the law, however, because – unlike a state's coercion of its constitutents – it is not true that perilous circumstances would inevitably prevail unless I obey the law. Indeed, an average citizen's (dis)obedience typically has no discernible effect whatsoever upon a government's capacity to perform its functions, so it appears that no strictly consequential account of our duty to obey the state's commands can be plausible. To emphasize: In order for a samaritan account of the duty to obey the law to work, it would have to be true that others would be imperiled were it not for my legal compliance. But because there are plenty of cases in which no one (let alone all of my compatriots) would be any (let alone perilously) worse off if I disobeyed the law, it is unclear how samaritanism is relevant here. Given these facts, one might be tempted to jettison the samaritan approach. As I will now argue, however, these observations about necessity demonstrate only that we must further refine the samaritan account to take account of the social nature of the solution to the perils of the state of nature.

Rather than reject samaritanism as the key to explaining our duty to obey the law, I recommend that we merely import the nonconsequential consideration of fairness. Thus, while it is certainly true that states rather than individual persons are necessary and sufficient to eliminate the perils of the state of nature, we must not lose sight of the fact that a state is nothing more than the (coerced) coordination of numerous individual persons. Moreover, we must bear in mind that a state's capacity to perform its functions (and the amount of sacrifice required by the state's constituents) depends principally upon the percentage of those subjects who comply with the state's legal commands. Finally, because the responsibility to rescue others from peril falls equally upon all of us, I suggest that we understand our political obligations as our fair share of the communal samaritan chore of rescuing others from the perils of the state of nature. On this view, each of us is bound to obey the law because all of us have a responsibility to help rescue others when this assistance is not unreasonably costly.

At this point, a critic might object that this samaritan approach will not suffice because it cannot explain why one's fair share of rescuing others from peril must come in the form of obedience to the law. In other words, even if one assumes that each of us has a responsibility to rescue others from peril, there are numerous people facing various types of dangers all over the world, so it is not clear why the mandate that we do our fair share to help those in peril requires us to obey the law rather than, say, send money to famine relief. This objection (which emphasizes what John Simmons has called the "particularity requirement") is especially powerful because it promises to undermine the account offered here *even if one concedes everything I have asserted to this point.*[3] In other words, this form of criticism seems on target even if it is true that (1) states supply vital benefits that would not be available in their absence, (2) states perform their requisite functions without imposing unreasonable costs on their subjects, (3) samaritan duties exist, and (4) considerations of fairness can explain why we must do our fair share in support of communal samaritan projects. To fully appreciate the force of this objection, it is important to understand the particularity requirement and why critics have invoked it to challenge other accounts of our political obligations.

The Particularity Requirement

The particularity requirement became prominent in the literature when Simmons raised it in response to those who argued that our duty to obey the law should be understood as a natural duty. Conceiving of the duty to obey the law as a natural duty to support just institutions was welcomed as a great advance because it promised to explain why everyone, regardless of her transactional or associative history, is obligated to comply with the state's legal commands.[4] The central idea is that because justice is such

---

3 Simmons introduced the particularity requirement in *Moral Principles and Political Obligations,* especially in Chapters II and VI.

4 One's transactional history is a function of the things done by and for one, like the promises one has made, the favors one has done for others, the benefits one has received, and so on. One's associative history is constituted by the socially significant associations one has had with friends, family members, colleagues, compatriots, and such.

an important value, it stands to reason that each of us has a duty
to promote it. And because institutions often play such a pivotal
and ineliminable role in making the world a more just place, the
mandate to promote justice should be understood in terms of supporting just institutions. Thus, by beginning with a natural duty,
defenders of this account need posit neither a previous transaction nor a preexisting association to explain why each of us is
bound. Problems remain, however, because it is not clear why
the general duty to support just institutions must be cashed out
in terms of the more particularized obligation to obey the laws
of one's own state. Even if one assumes that governments are
just institutions, for instance, what explains why we must support them rather than other, nonpolitical institutions designed to
make the world more just? And even if we must support political states, why must each person support her own state? Why is
each of us not free to support either the just state of her choosing
or perhaps the most just state, for instance? Finally, even if we
could somehow establish that each person is specifically bound
to support her own state, it remains to be explained why this
support must come in the form of faithful obedience to the law;
why are we not free to choose the manner in which we support
our governments?

Thus, while natural duty theories enjoy an initial advantage
over those accounts that rely upon a historical transaction or association, they are vulnerable to a distinctive type of objection.
Transactional and associative approaches have had trouble establishing the requisite historical act/relationship, but at least it is
clear to whom one is bound: the transactee/associate. Natural
duty theorists need show no historical act/relationship, but then
it remains mysterious to whom in particular one is bound. Natural duty theorists would be well positioned to meet this challenge
if they began by assuming a natural duty either to *support all just
institutions in precisely the form that they request to be supported* or,
more specifically, to *obey the law*. The former is too ambitious to
be plausible, however, and the latter *assumes* rather than *explains*
political obligation. Thus, the operative challenge for any natural duty theorist is to begin with a sufficiently modest, intuitively

compelling natural duty and yet still show how this plausible general imperative requires one to perform the highly particularized chore of obeying the laws of one's own country.

In light of the preceding discussion, it should be apparent why the samaritan approach must contend with the particularity requirement. Insofar as my account of our duty to obey the law features samaritanism, it clearly relies upon a natural duty. Samaritan duties are natural because they do not depend upon a previous transaction or a preexisting association between the rescuer and the rescuee; if a person is sufficiently imperiled and one can save her at no unreasonable cost, one cannot justify one's failure to rescue by pointing out that one never agreed to do so or that one had no morally significant relationship with her, for instance. Moreover, I regard the fact that samaritan duties are widely accepted in a variety of contexts as ample evidence that they provide just the type of modest, intuitively compelling moral foundation upon which we should seek to construct a generally acceptable account of our duty to obey the law. However, while samaritan duties are attractive insofar as few people are pretheoretically inclined to doubt their existence, like other natural duties they must contend with the particularity requirement. More specifically, once one recognizes both that people experience various types of peril and that samaritan duties can be owed to anyone, at least three pressing questions emerge. First, given that political instability is by no means the only source of peril, why can we insist that our share of samaritan assistance must come in the form of helping to supply *political* benefits as opposed to providing nonpolitical benefits, as one would if one contributed to famine relief, for instance? Second, even if one can establish that one must contribute to the avoidance of political instability, what explains why this contribution must be made to one's own country? Given that samaritan duties do not depend upon the existence of a socially salient relationship (and thus do not depend upon the fact that one's *compatriots* might become imperiled), it is difficult to see why samaritanism would require one to support one's own country. Finally, even if it could be shown that one must support one's own state in particular, what explains why this support must come in the currency of compliance with one's government's legal commands? Merely obeying the law is not always the most effective way to support one's country, so it is not entirely clear why obedience to the law should be singled out as that which is invariably demanded. In short, although it does not seem terribly controversial to suggest that all of us have a moral duty to do our share to rescue others from grave peril, it is far from clear how this general mandate requires us in particular to obey the laws of our own state. Addressing these admittedly difficult questions in order, I will suggest that each can be answered once one recognizes the significance of two facts: (1) political instability creates a coordination problem and (2) discretion is a good.

Let us first explore why doing one's fair share to rescue others from peril necessarily requires one to support *political* institutions. For instance, why is it that I could not do my share by contributing substantially to groups like Oxfam America, which assist starving people in famine-stricken countries? Indeed, given that my compatriots' political peril is merely potential, whereas the peril of those currently starving to death is actual, if anything it seems as though samaritanism would require me to withhold my U.S. taxes in order to send the money instead to famine relief. Thus, not only is it mysterious how an account built upon samaritan duties could single out political obligations, it appears that it might actually recommend that we neglect our political responsibilities to attend to far more pressing issues (like acquired immune deficiency syndrome [AIDS] and famine) that currently pose more grave peril.

Although I think that those of us in wealthy countries do far too little to address the various types of nonpolitical peril that claim so many lives around the world, I nonetheless believe that political peril is distinctive in two important ways. First, whatever one might do to eliminate nonpolitical peril will not excuse one from doing one's share to eliminate political peril. In other words, it is not possible to earn "credits" in other arenas that would excuse one from doing one's share in the political realm; thus someone like Mother Teresa could not justify her legal disobedience by claiming that she paid her portion of the samaritan bill at the

Calcutta office, for instance. Second, while we might have a responsibility to eliminate various types of nonpolitical peril, only political states are justified in *forcing* us to do our share. Thus, whereas my government might justifiably threaten to punish me if I disobey the law, Oxfam America would not be justified in punishing me if I chose not to contribute to this organization. The crucial distinguishing feature of political peril is that it is not merely a big problem, it is fundamentally a *coordination* problem.

I say that political instability is fundamentally a coordination problem because there is no way effectively to eliminate the sources of this type of peril without coordinating people. As emphasized earlier, harmful chaos would prevail unless virtually all of those in spatial proximity defer to the same set of clearly defined rules. Other types of peril, like famine or disease, could be just as big and dangerous as political instability, but they are not essentially problems of coordination because coordination need not be necessary for their solution. Consider world hunger, for instance. It is an open empirical question whether Bill Gates has sufficient funds to buy the food necessary to effectively eliminate famine, but there is no reason in theory why he could not do so. It is clearly not an empirical question whether Gates has enough money to eradicate the peril caused by political instability, however, because the latter is not the type of problem that can be satisfactorily addressed with money alone. Even if Gates had half of the money in the world, for instance, he could not ensure political stability either abroad or at home because peace and justice are not the types of goods that can be single-handedly secured by an individual; they prevail only when virtually everyone defers to the same authority. The fact that political peril is inherently a problem of coordination is important because it helps explain why political coercion can be justified. It is not merely that political coercion is a *possible* solution to the harmful circumstances of the state of nature; it is the *only* viable solution because only coordination will solve the problems, and there is no way to ensure sufficient coordination without coercion. Thus, my state permissibly coerces me because uniform coercion within its borders is the only solution.

To appreciate the importance of this point, compare my state to Oxfam America, which (let us assume) does an admirable job of raising funds and distributing vital resources to some of the world's most imperiled people. At first blush, it might seem that Oxfam could run an analogous argument: It should be allowed to take my funds without my permission in order to feed people who would otherwise starve to death. Upon closer inspection, however, there is a telling disanalogy between my state and Oxfam. It may be true that coercing me would be a viable way to raise the funds required to save more imperiled people, but it is clearly not the *only* way to do so. There are various ways to raise the funds without coercing me because the funds could come from anywhere. The crucial point is that there is nothing special about *my* money – funds from Bill Gates or anyone else would be just as effective. Because political instability is a coordination problem that must be solved territorially, on the other hand, there is something about those in the relevant territory that singles them out as special. Think of it this way: A state could not perform its requisite functions merely by coercing a large number of randomly chosen, physically discontiguous people (as it would if it coerced all of the world's red-haired people or everyone whose last name begins with the letter **W**, for instance) because peace and stability require not just that people be coordinated but that those who *regularly interact* with one another (i.e., those who are spatially contiguous) all play by the same rules. Thus, whereas Oxfam could function just as well whether it received funds from me or from someone living on another continent, my country is obviously not indifferent between the prospects of coercing me or someone living elsewhere in the world. As a consequence, advocating the samaritan account does not require a theorist implausibly to suggest that political chaos is the only (or even the worst) type of peril in the world; one can admit that the world sadly contains a variety of sources of extreme peril and yet still single out political peril as distinctive insofar as it can be solved only via coordination. And since the sufficient level of coordination cannot be achieved without coercion, this explains why we can consistently defend political coercion without thereby committing ourselves to the conclusion that groups like Oxfam, which also rescue people from peril, may permissibly employ similar types of coercion.

Even if the preceding reasoning is on target, and there are good reasons to single out political states as uniquely justified in coercing their constituents, this is only the first step in addressing the particularity requirement. More work remains to be done because the arguments just offered are a potential justification for the *state's* uninvited imposition, but they do not in themselves establish that individual citizens have an obligation to obey the law. The particularity requirement has not yet been satisfied because the distinction between a government and organizations like Oxfam depends upon the *necessity* of the former coercing its own constituents in particular and, as emphasized earlier, a single citizen's political obedience is not typically *necessary* in the way that an entire state's presence is. To emphasize: Even if political states are uniquely justified in coercing their constituents because such coercion is the only way that they can perform their requisite (samaritan) functions, this does not establish that any given citizen's duty to do her fair share of rescuing others from peril must come in the form of obedience to her state's legal commands. To reiterate the salient questions that remain unanswered: Even if one has a duty to do one's fair share of assisting those in peril, why must this share include supporting political institutions? And even if one must support political institutions, why must one in particular support that institution currently imposing itself on one? And finally, even if one must support one's own country, why must this support come in the particular form of obedience to the law? As I shall now explain, these three related questions can be satisfactorily answered, but only once one recognizes that discretion is a good of which one may not take more than one's fair share.

Let us begin with the most general of these three questions: Why does the duty to do one's fair share of assisting those in peril require one more specifically to support political institutions? To appreciate the force of this question, think again of Mother Teresa. Given that Mother Teresa did so much to help gravely imperiled strangers, why was her monumental sacrifice not sufficient to discharge any samaritan duty that one might reasonably posit? More to the point, how can I suggest that, in addition to everything else she did to help those in pain, her duty to do her fair share of rescuing others from peril also required her to support political institutions?

Answering this question requires combining the fact that political chaos presents a coordination problem with the observation that discretion is a good. I do not take myself to be asserting anything terribly insightful or controversial in proclaiming discretion to be a good; I understand this simply as the commonsensical idea that each of us has good reason to want to be the author of our own lives, to choose the types of things on which we expend time and energy, and to be the one who determines which causes we support. To give just a few of the more obvious examples, we would like to decide for ourselves which (if any) religion to practice, which (if any) profession to pursue, which (if any) people with whom to associate, and which (if any) hobbies to explore. Discretion's status as a good is relevant to our duty to obey the law because virtually all of us would like to have discretion as to how we contribute our fair share to rescuing others. Imagine, for instance, that Bill, Catharine, Peter, Ted, and Teresa all live on my street. As it turns out, all five of my neighbors are extremely virtuous, and thus each is more than happy to act as morality requires, including doing his or her fair share to rescue others from peril. It should come as no surprise, however, that each has very different interests and inclinations, and thus each is disposed to support different worthy projects. Thus, Ted donates heavily to the United Nations, Bill contributes large sums to those stricken with human immunodeficiency virus (HIV)/AIDS, Catharine works tirelessly to reduce the amount of sexual violence, Peter dedicates himself to both persuading the relatively wealthy to give money to the poorest people in the world and to arguing on behalf of vulnerable animals, and Teresa toils endlessly on behalf of those starving to death. None of them, however, is particularly impressed with the benefits governments provide, and thus none contributes to the elimination of political peril. That is, Ted, Bill, Catharine, Peter, and Teresa are all very generous people who contribute a great deal to the welfare of others, but none faithfully obeys the law or pays taxes.

What would you say about my neighbors? Would you insist that they are to be applauded for having done much more than I? Or do you think that they should be criticized for disobeying the law? My own view is that while my neighbors are to be praised for their exemplary generosity, they are also to be morally criticized for their disregard for the authority of the law. It might seem inconsistent for someone who conceives of the duty to obey the law as a samaritan chore to single out these people as especially committed to rescuing others from peril and yet simultaneously to object to their failure to obey the law, but the apparent inconsistency dissolves once one notices that my neighbors have helped themselves to more than their fair share of discretion. Teresa, for instance, attends to those starving to death because she is moved by famine victims, and Bill donates large sums to help those infected with HIV/AIDS because he is especially interested in this particular cause. But notice that Teresa, Bill, and my three other neighbors are able to disregard our state's legal commands only because the rest of us *do* respect the state's authority. More importantly, the rest of us would also prefer to ignore our government's legal commands in order to focus our attention more fully on the particular causes about which we feel most passionately, but the consequences would be catastrophic if all of us did so. In other words, my five neighbors are free riders *even though they are doing more than the rest of us* because they are enjoying the good of discretion, a good that is available only because the rest of us obey the law. Of course, the fact that these neighbors free ride on our obedience to the law does not erase the fact that they are incredibly generous to the causes about which they care, and thus there is nothing inconsistent about acknowledging their extraordinary generosity on the one hand and criticizing them for wrongly taking advantage of the rest of us on the other. Thus, as much as we might applaud Mother Teresa for doing so much on behalf of the famine-stricken in Calcutta, for instance, we would also be right to criticize her legal disobedience. The bottom line, then, is that obedience to the law is not just one more way that one might choose to do one's fair share of rescuing others from peril. It is uniquely mandatory because legal solutions are fundamentally coordination mechanisms that are predicated on each of us forgoing our individual discretion.

This account of what is special about political institutions paves the way to our responses to the second and third questions about our particular political responsibilities because, once one recognizes what is distinctive about political institutions, it is not difficult to appreciate why one must support one's own state and why this support must come in the form of obedience to the government's legal commands. The short answer, in both cases, is that one's fair share must come in this particular currency because we could not effectively eliminate the peril if each person retained discretion regarding which government to support and how to support it. It is worth elaborating a bit on this brief answer.

Recall that the second question we must answer is, even if doing one's fair share to rescue others from peril requires one to support the elimination of political peril, why may each of us not choose which government to support? If I happen to think that Canada's government is the most just, for instance, then why may I not withhold my taxes from the United States in order to send the money to my neighbors to the north? Moreover, even if the samaritan account would require me to support one government in particular, it is not obvious that this would always be my own government. Given that the obligation in question purportedly stems from the importance of saving imperiled strangers, if I were required to send my money to one country in particular, it would seem more appropriate that I should give it to whichever state has the most precarious political arrangement (as I write this, Haiti comes to mind). If I sent my money to Canada (or Haiti), then I am certainly doing as much as I would have done in merely paying my taxes (and, unlike the hypothetical Mother Teresa, I cannot be accused of failing to do my share to eliminate *political* peril), so why have I not fulfilled my obligation to do my fair share to rescue others from peril?

The answer to this question becomes apparent when we reflect upon what would happen if *everyone* were given the discretion to choose which government to support. It takes little imagination to see that governments would have considerable difficulties securing peace and protecting basic moral rights if they could count on the financial support and legal obedience of only those constituents who freely chose to support the government presiding over them. (And even if some governments could somehow function effectively, they would have to demand considerably more of those citizens who willingly supported them.) In other words, the "solution" of requiring merely that everyone contribute to the promotion of political stability in whichever fashion she sees fit would be no solution at all because governments could not in fact function effectively if everyone had this discretion. Thus, the reason I may not withhold my U.S. taxes in order to contribute to the government of Canada or Haiti is that my doing so would involve helping myself to a type of discretion that could not be enjoyed by everyone. Obviously I would prefer to have this discretion, but it would be unfair to reserve it for myself when my doing so depends upon others being denied this very same good.

Finally, it should now be apparent that the same line of reasoning used to answer our first two questions can also help us respond to our third question: Even if each of us must support her own government, why must this support come in terms of compliance with the state's legal commands? Why are we not free to support our government however we would like, perhaps by paying more than our fair share of taxes, working overtime to encourage people to vote, or dedicating time to encourage fidelity to those particular laws about which we feel most strongly? Once again, the reason each person cannot be left free to choose the form in which she will support her state is that governments could not function effectively if everyone enjoyed this discretion. The fact that states solve a coordination problem is again paramount here: The key function of states is to get everyone in the given territory to defer to a single definitive set of rules, so obviously a government could not perform this function unless it required each of us to follow these rules. Now, because most of us typically disagree with at least some of our state's laws, clearly we would prefer to be able to choose which laws to obey or perhaps to offer our support in some fashion that has nothing to do with obedience to these rules. But since a few of us could reserve this discretion for ourselves only against a backdrop of general compliance in which others are denied this discretion, clearly it would be wrong to unfairly make an exception for ourselves.

To review: Although there would likely be no discernible consequence if a typical citizen either (1) failed to contribute to political stability, (2) contributed to some foreign state rather than her own, or (3) contributed to her own state in some fashion other than obedience to its laws, disregarding the law would still be impermissible because legal obedience is required as one's fair share of helping to rescue others from peril. It seems awkward to say that a legally disobedient citizen can fail to do her fair share of samaritan rescues even if (like Mother Teresa) she dedicates dramatically more of her time and energy to those people who are most imperiled, but the distinctive nature of political peril makes this moral condemnation appropriate. The key point is not merely that Teresa and my other imagined neighbors could not effectively pursue their favored samaritan projects in the absence of political stability, nor is it that the perils of the state of nature are always the most pressing. The point, rather, is that the perils that prevail in the absence of political society are distinct insofar as they create what is fundamentally a coordination problem: There is no way other than general compliance with a single authoritative set of rules to secure peace and protect basic moral rights. The upshot of this is not only that we must sacrifice to rescue others from the perils of the state of nature, but also that we (as individuals) *have essentially no discretion as to the form that our sacrifice must take.* Of course, virtually all of us would prefer to determine the content of our sacrifice, but the political solution to the perils of the state of nature is predicated on denying individuals this sort of dominion, so an integral part of the sacrifice is to have little to no say in what our sacrifice must be. If one reserves for oneself this individual dominion (by ignoring the law so that one might contribute more to some apolitical peril, by contributing to political stability elsewhere, or even by contributing to one's own state in an extralegal manner), then one is helping oneself to an unfair portion of discretion, free riding on others who have forgone this discretion.

None of this is to suggest that apolitical peril does not exist or that there are no moral reasons to ameliorate it. Clearly, we should care deeply about those who are starving to death or suffering with various poverty-related diseases, and equally clearly, one is virtuous to the extent that one sacrifices on behalf of these people. But the crucial point is that each of us enjoys a degree of discretion regarding these other types of peril that we lack with respect to political peril. Whereas one is generally free to choose which charitable causes to support, one has a duty to obey the law because this type of discretion is incompatible with solving the dire coordination problem that the state of nature presents. Thus, even though the samaritan account of our duty to obey the law begins with a natural duty, it can satisfy the particularity requirement because there is a straightforward explanation for why our duty to do our fair share to rescue others from peril must come in the particular form of obedience to the laws of one's own state.

Particularity and Citizenship

At this point, a critic might object that even if the samaritan theory can explain why one has a duty to obey the laws of the state presiding over one's territory, this is not sufficient to satisfy the particularity requirement because this requirement includes other, more demanding conditions. Indeed, as Simmons describes the problem of particularity, it is not enough to demonstrate how a general duty can require one to obey the laws of one's own state; one must also offer a "principle of political obligation which binds the citizen to one particular state above all others, namely that state in which he is a citizen."[5]

In other words, even if samaritanism can explain why one has an obligation to obey the law wherever one travels, it appears incapable of capturing the special ties one has to one's compatriots

5 Simmons, *Moral Principles and Political Obligations*, 31–2.

and one's own country. To appreciate the force of this problem, consider the situation of those who travel abroad. The samaritan theory of our duty to obey the law (rightly, I think) implies that Paul from Canada has a duty to obey the Australian laws when he travels to Australia, for instance, but most of us think that Paul continues to have a moral obligation to pay his Canadian taxes even if he lives in Australia for an extended period of time. It is unclear how any theory based on samaritan duties can explain this latter duty, however, because samaritanism appears indifferent to any relationship between a person and her compatriots or state. First and most obviously, since samaritan duties are by definition owed to moral strangers (i.e., they exist independently of any previous transaction or preexisting association), they appear ill equipped to explain why Paul owes more to Canadians than to Australians. Second and just as importantly, because I have argued that samaritanism particularizes one's political duties territorially, it is unclear how this approach could possibly suggest that a Canadian living abroad can retain a special duty to Canada. Indeed, given that I have insisted that political states can perform their requisite political functions only if they uniformly coerce all those who are territorially contiguous (and thus, peace could not be secured if citizens were sorted into separate countries according to eye color, or even according to place of birth if sufficient numbers of people were transient, for instance), it seems that I must also insist that whatever duties Paul initially had to the state of Canada would immediately be owed to the Australian government once his plane lands in Australia.

Because I think there is something to this more demanding construal of the particularity requirement, let us explore how a samaritan theorist might go about explaining the special relationship between expatriates like Paul and their territorially distant states. Before doing so, however, I want to stress that we need not reject the samaritan theory even if it proved utterly incompatible with the special moral bonds pretheoretically thought to exist among compatriots and between a citizen and her state. There are two related reasons that samaritanism should be retained even if it cannot satisfy the most stringent construal of the particularity requirement. First, by far the most pressing challenge in political theory is to explain the twin convictions that (1) political states may legitimately coerce their subjects and (2) constituents have a moral duty to obey these coercive laws. It is also true that many of us are pretheoretically inclined to posit a special, morally salient relationship between a citizen and her state, but this relationship is unquestionably secondary to the core political issues of state legitimacy and political obligation. Thus, it would be wrong to reject a theory merely because it could not accommodate *all* of our pretheoretic intuitions; instead, we should value the samaritan approach for the straightforward fashion in which it answers our most important questions. (Just as we abandon a scientific theory only when we have a better one, not merely because it cannot explain all the data, in political philosophy we should not dismiss samaritanism merely because it is not obvious how it squares with every pretheoretic conviction.) Secondly, notice that our belief in the special relationship between a citizen and her state is not only of secondary importance, it is also held with less conviction. While most of us come to the subject with a variety of beliefs about our political duties, we are typically by far the most confident in our two most basic suppositions that a state may permissibly coerce those within its territory and that constituents have a duty to defer to those rules. As a consequence, first and foremost we should seek a theory of political obligation that squares with our two most confident judgments. Thus, rather than discard an account if it could accommodate only these beliefs, we should remain open to revising some of our less confident antecedent judgments if they appear unjustified by the best theories. Thus, for two reasons I think it would be unwise to place too much importance on a theory's capacity to satisfy the most demanding version of the particularity requirement. As I mentioned earlier, however, I share the pretheoretic view that not all political obligations must be territorially grounded, so let me now explain how an advocate of samaritanism might describe Paul's special political obligations to Canada and Canadians.

To begin, let me acknowledge that it is not at all clear how samaritanism on its own could explain a citizen's special moral bond to her territorially distant state or compatriots. It does not follow that defenders of the samaritan approach must deny these additional moral responsibilities, however, because there is obviously more to ethics than samaritanism, and nothing prohibits a samaritan theorist from invoking these other moral considerations as long as they are not incompatible with samaritanism. After all, the arguments to this point have not been designed to show that nonsamaritan considerations are always beside the point; rather, I have sought to show only that an account grounded in samaritanism can explain our moral duty to obey the law.

Here a critic might object that it is wrong to invoke nonsamaritan considerations at this stage on the grounds that, if various transactional and associative considerations were not acceptable earlier, presumably they should be just as problematic now. This objection is misguided, however, because it implies that the moral landscape cannot evolve in significant ways. In particular, once samaritan-justified states are in existence, their presence might subsequently give rise to morally relevant relations either among fellow citizens or between citizens and their states. For example, many insist that states cannot be legitimate unless governed democratically. If this is correct, then there may be requirements of effective democracy (which have nothing to do with samaritanism) that explain either why the state must be ordered in some particular fashion or why compatriots must treat each other in a given manner. Similarly, if equality is an essentially relational matter (so that the permissibility of any given inequality depends upon the relationship between the haves and have-nots), then it might follow that compatriots have greater redistributive responsibilities to one another than to otherwise similarly situated foreigners.

It is not essential to pursue these and other possibilities further here; for now, I would like to stress the voluntary nature of citizenship for expatriates like Paul. Specifically, if it is plausible to suppose that someone like Paul has an obligation to continue paying his Canadian taxes even though he now lives in Australia, it is because he *chooses* to retain his citizenship. If Paul wanted to have nothing to do with Canada (or even if he merely felt that retaining his Canadian citizenship was not worth the costs), then he could simply renounce his citizenship. And given that Paul has the option to avoid altogether the costs and benefits of Canadian citizenship, it seems reasonable to regard whatever costs he incurs as voluntarily accepted.

At this point, one might object that consent cannot ground Paul's obligation for the very reasons I dismissed consent-based accounts of our duty to obey the law in Chapter 1. This objection misses the mark, though, because my earlier contention that *not everyone* has consented to the state's presence does not entail that *no one* has. More specifically, earlier I questioned the consent theory of our duty to obey the law because states could not satisfactorily perform their requisite functions if they coerced only those who freely consented. It does not follow from this, however, that no one has so agreed. Among those who appear to have consented, two groups stand out: naturalized citizens, who make an explicit agreement when they enter the territory, and expatriates, who choose to retain their citizenship when they leave the country. (It is no coincidence that these two groups consist of individuals who freely cross the state's territorial borders.)

A critic might also protest that it is wrong to characterize Paul's retention of citizenship as fully voluntary because the costs of severing his connection with Canada are potentially dire, especially if he cannot immediately become an Australian citizen. Indeed, given how vulnerable one might be if one had no citizenship, it is tempting to understand Paul's choice to retain allegiance to Canada as coerced. And since coerced choices are typically not morally binding, it seems inappropriate to suggest that Paul's political duties to Canada are justified by being voluntarily incurred. I resist this potential objection as well, however, because the extraordinary benefits of citizenship need not coerce an expatriate to remain a citizen any more than a car's great utility coerces its owner to retain ownership. (Indeed, if anything, this objection merely confirms the point I have emphasized throughout: that the net costs of political life cannot be characterized as unreasonably burdensome.) Thus, it strikes me as perfectly sensible to suggest that samaritan considerations justify the state's presence in relation to all of those within its territory (even those who have not consented and would prefer to take their chances in a state of nature), and that territorially distant expatriates might also have a moral duty to incur the costs of citizenship when they voluntarily retain their standing as citizens.

Finally, I should acknowledge a striking limitation to my suggestion that Paul's continued responsibilities to Canada are voluntarily incurred: It does not explain how Paul might be bound to Canada *even if he renounced his citizenship*. In other words, by fastening upon the voluntary acceptance of political ties, I apparently have no way to explain why *all* expatriates have a special obligation to their "home" states, regardless of their personal interest in retaining their original citizenship.

There are two salient ways to respond to this limitation: Either I could search for other, nonvoluntary grounds for the special moral ties each of us has to her state, or I could simply embrace this limitation as appropriate. Although I do not deny that there could occasionally be morally relevant considerations that entail that various expatriates have an enduring, nonvoluntary debt to their countries, I am more inclined toward the second option. In my view, it is no counterexample to the samaritan account that it does not necessarily imply that Paul has an irrevocable duty to Canada. On the contrary, even if some of us have a vague pretheoretic sense that we all have permanent, nonterritorial, and nonvoluntary duties to the states in which we are born and/or raised, I think this belief should be abandoned. To suggest that a state enjoys a permanent position of moral dominion over all of those it unilaterally claims as citizens (even if these people deliberately move out of the territory and explicitly renounce their citizenship) is tantamount to conceiving of citizens as essentially the political property of their states. I assume without argument that this position is implausible. Moreover, even if an occasional theorist is inclined to endorse such a radical position, certainly voluntarists who are skeptical that we have *any* political obligations would not reject my account for its failure to give states such an extreme and irrevocable claim over their citizens. Indeed, to put the point in a stark but revealing context, I began this book by arguing at length that citizenship is importantly distinct from slavery, so it should come as no surprise that I now deny that states enjoy a type of claim over their constituents that slave owners mistook themselves as having over their slaves.

To review, it seems right that samaritan considerations on their own cannot accommodate all of our pretheoretic intuitions about our political obligations, but this is no cause for concern both because they appear capable of explaining our duty to obey the law and because there is no reason why they cannot be combined with other morally relevant considerations that help explain other facts, such as why (some) expatriates have a duty to pay taxes to their country of citizenship. It appears true that even a suitably supplemented samaritanism could not explain every political duty that some are inclined to posit, but I take this as a virtue rather than a deficiency of the account. Clearly, the appropriate goal is not to explain every political responsibility ever conceived, but rather to justify those duties that, on reflection, seem plausible to assert. In terms of our more specific discussion, we should conclude that even if citizens can on occasion find themselves with moral duties to which they did not freely consent, citizenship is emphatically *not* tantamount to slavery, and we should be judicious about positing extreme and irrevocable duties as well as wary of those who do.

Conclusion

Some of us may have political duties grounded in consent, and many of us might have a duty to obey the law in return for the political benefits that we have received, but if the arguments to this point have been sound, then samaritan considerations form the foundation of a theory that explains why all of us have a moral duty to comply with the state's legal commands.[6] Let me emphasize, however, that at no point have I meant to suggest

6 For the most thorough and sophisticated defenses of the consent and fairness theories of the duty to obey the law, see Harry Beran, *The Consent Theory of Political Obligation* (London: Croom Helm, 1987), and George Klosko, *The Principle of Fairness and Political Obligations* (Lanham, MD: Rowman & Littlefield, 1992).

that we *invariably* have an *absolute* moral duty to obey the law. On the contrary, I seek to show only that there is a prima facie obligation to obey the *just* laws of a *legitimate* regime. Spelling out my thesis in this way indicates that our account will not be complete until we have said something about (1) which laws are just, (2) when a state is legitimate, and (3) how and when a prima facie obligation to obey the law might be overridden. With this in mind, I will turn next to questions regarding which laws are just, and in the fourth and final chapter I will reflect on how one should respond when confronted with either an unjust law or an illegitimate regime. For now, we can conclude at most that we all have a defeasible moral duty to follow a just law validly enacted by a legitimate regime.

3   Just and Unjust Laws

G IVEN my specification that we have a moral duty to obey only the just laws of a legitimate regime, it is natural to explore what types of laws are in fact just. This matter is especially pressing for those who draw on samaritanism because a critic might worry that samaritan considerations are too restricted to justify most of the functions that modern bureaucratic states legitimately perform. In particular, samaritanism appears incapable of justifying all those functions that either require extremely costly sacrifices or do not rescue anyone from peril. To show how an advocate of samaritanism might respond to this challenge, this chapter focuses on two types of laws: those that require citizens to vote and those that draft citizens into compulsory military service. In the end, I conclude that an approach based on samaritanism has more resources to explain governmental functions than might initially be apparent, but that we should nonetheless be open to the possibility that many of the practices of existing states, even liberal democratic ones, are entirely unjustified.

Even if samaritan considerations cannot justify many of the functions that modern bureaucratic states regularly assign themselves, there are two reasons not to dismiss the approach on these grounds. First, as I mentioned in the previous chapter, there is no reason why defenders of the samaritan approach cannot appeal to other considerations that justify various additional obligations. The crucial point is that, once samaritan-justified states are in place, their presence may well change the political landscape in morally relevant ways. If compatriots have special redistributive responsibilities to one another, for instance, these duties need not (and apparently could not) be explained solely in terms of samaritanism.[1] Instead, presumably something like a morally relevant feature of their shared citizenship would be required to explain why compatriots owe more to one another than to unrelated foreigners. Such an account would not render samaritanism irrelevant (samaritanism would remain essential to explaining why states are justified in the first place), but it would suggest that many of our political duties might be best understood as arising from morally relevant relations that obtain only after states have been constructed.[2]

A second reason not to summarily dismiss samaritanism for its apparent inability to justify all of the actions performed by modern bureaucratic states is that many of these actions may actually be unjustified. It is common to criticize contemporary states for failing to do *enough* (people regularly condemn the United States for not guaranteeing even a minimal level of health care for all of its citizens, for instance), but it may be that existing states equally deserve criticism for doing *too* much. If so, then it is at least worth questioning whether those political duties that cannot be explained by samaritanism (or other plausible considerations) are genuine. Indeed, I focus here on the duties to vote and to serve in the military precisely because these two obligations – though regularly taken for granted – are surprisingly difficult to justify. If the grounds for these putative obligations can be found, then there is no antecedent reason to assume that an advocate of the samaritan theory cannot simply embrace the relevant arguments. If we are ultimately unable to generate a plausible account of these duties, on the other hand, this obviously should not lead us to reject samaritanism. On the contrary, it would seem more appropriate to reconsider whether these duties are genuine after all.

1 On the question of special obligations among compatriots, see my "Relational Facts in Liberal Political Theory: Is There Magic in the Pronoun 'My'?" *Ethics* 110 (2000): 537–62.
2 For an excellent discussion of how multiple considerations might be combined to explain various political duties, see George Klosko, "Multiple Principles of Political Obligation," *Political Theory* 32 (2004): 801–24.

(And even if one could not bear to question these duties, the inability to adequately defend them gives us no reason to single out the samaritan account as particularly problematic.)

Although I will question the genuineness of both the duty to vote and the duty to serve in the military, my principal concern is not to construct a conclusive argument against their existence. My chief aim is more general. What I most hope the reader will take away from this chapter is a heightened awareness that states may be routinely inserting themselves into matters where their presence is not justified. If this is accurate, then it may be a virtue rather than a liability of the samaritan theory that it requires a distinct explanation for the state's performance of any chore that is not necessary to rescue us from peril. Put another way, governments are not to be given carte blanche, and we should be suspicious of any theory that leaves us unable even to question the legitimacy of a state's imposition into the affairs of its constituents.

The Duty to Vote

It is widely accepted that citizens have a duty to vote, but it is far from clear how this obligation might be explained in terms of samaritanism. Although voting is typically not a demanding chore, it certainly does not appear to rescue anyone from peril. Quite the contrary; in all but the most exceptional circumstances, one's vote is almost certainly not going to decide the outcome and thus is likely to have no consequence whatsoever.

It is tempting to cite the 2000 U.S. presidential election as an obvious counterexample to the claim that one's vote is inconsequential, but this would be wrong for two reasons. First, in most states the margin of victory was enormous and never in question. In the state of Georgia, where I was living at the time, for instance, neither major candidate even bothered to campaign because both recognized that George W. Bush was sure to win the state. (Al Gore repeatedly flew into Atlanta for private fund-raisers, but he normally did not even pause to make a quick public appearance. Instead, he funneled the money raised in Atlanta into his campaigns in so-called battleground states where the decision was in question.) And if the candidates recognize that it is not worth their time to campaign in a given state (even when their fund-raising schedule repeatedly takes them there), then it is hard to see why individuals living in one of these states should believe that they have consequential reasons to expend their (admittedly minimal) energy to vote.

Second and more importantly, one cannot even say that the close race in Florida proves that every vote counts, despite the fact that only a few hundred votes would have changed the outcome in Florida, which in turn would have changed the overall out-come. Or, more accurately, it may be true that every vote counts, but this is beside the point because not every vote is *decisive*. In Florida in 2000, for instance, anyone who did not vote because she thought her vote would not make a difference need have no regrets because her vote would in fact have been inconsequen-tial. It is true that Florida's outcome was decided by only a few hundred votes, but individuals do not have a few hundred votes; they have only one. Thus, whether or not she voted, any given individual in Florida had no influence on the outcome. Admit-tedly, if the election had been similar on a national level and the outcome in Florida had been determined by one single vote, then everyone who voted and everyone who did not would have been right to see her decision as having a consequence, but that was not the case in Florida in 2000 and, of course, the chances of that actually happening in an election of that size are astronomically small.

None of this is to deny that multiple individuals did in fact play decisive roles in George W. Bush's being installed as pres-ident. Most obviously, George W. Bush, Al Gore, Ralph Nader, Bill Clinton, Monica Lewinsky, each of the five justices on the U.S. Supreme Court who sided with the majority in *Bush v. Gore*, and probably even the person who designed the infamous "butterfly" ballot in Palm Beach County are among those who acted in ways that, as individuals, almost certainly affected the outcome of the election. That is to say, it is highly likely that Al Gore would have become the forty-third president of the United States had any one of these individuals acted differently at crucial moments. But the fact that a number of individuals may have had a decisive effect upon the 2000 election does not support any conclusion about the duty to vote because none of these people could have changed the outcome by *voting* any differently. Except in the most extraordinary of circumstances, then, it simply seems irrational to think that one's vote will determine the outcome of a large election.[3]

It is not uncommon for defenders of the duty to vote to object that one's vote is consequential even when it does not decide the outcome because it matters *how many* people vote for or against a given candidate/law/proposal. I am not sure that this is correct. In fact, because of the 2000 election, I currently live in a country with a president who was installed after receiving a *minority* of the popular votes. Given the enormous political influence George W. Bush has wielded despite the fact that the popular majority voted against him, it is difficult to make the case that one's margin of victory significantly affects the political climate after the election. (Interestingly, Bill Clinton, Bush's immediate predecessor, provides different reasons for skepticism. President Clinton was said to have enjoyed a huge "mandate" from the American people when he won such a large number [379 of 538] of the Electoral College votes in the 1996 presidential election. But because less than half of Americans voted – and because those who did were divided among three candidates – only about 24 percent of voting-age Americans actually voted for Clinton.) Most importantly, however, even if these cases are anomalous and the margin of victory/defeat is usually of consequence, this could not establish a duty to vote because each of us has only a single vote, and it strains credulity to assert that it matters whether a candidate wins or loses by *one more vote*. Clinton's putative mandate in 1996 stemmed from his garnering a disproportionate share of the Electoral College vote, for instance, and no single voter in

---

3 Loren E. Lomasky and Geoffrey Brennan provide a much more thorough and rigorous explanation of why voting in large elections is inconsequential in their excellent article "Is There a Duty to Vote?" *Social Philosophy & Policy* 17 (2000): 62–86.

any state could have changed that. Perhaps Clinton would have been less powerful if Bob Dole or Ross Perot had garnered several million more votes, but, again, an individual does not have several million votes. Each of us has only one vote, and thus there do not seem to be consequential reasons to vote even if it is true that the margin of victory/defeat sometimes makes a difference.

The standard rejoinder to the preceding observations is "What if everyone reasoned that way? What if no one voted?" I actually think that there is an important kernel of truth embedded in this reaction, but first, let me explain why this response does not suffice as it stands.

There is no question that one's vote could be enormously influential if *no one* else voted, but it is not clear what relevance this counterfactual thought experiment has for an individual acting in the real world, where huge numbers of people do vote. In other words, since a single individual's vote would indeed be decisive if no one else voted, it would be easy to construct a consequential argument for voting in such a world. But because we do not live in this world, it is unclear what relevance this observation has for those hoping to construct a consequential argument for the duty to vote. All is not lost, however, because I think the telling motivation behind objecting "What if everyone reasoned that way?" is to invoke *nonconsequential* considerations. That is, perhaps one can concede that voting in large elections is virtually certain to be inconsequential, but one can insist that one's duty to vote stems from the nonconsequential consideration of fairness.[4] Just as fairness is essential to explaining one's duty to obey the law, for instance, it may be the key to justifying the duty to vote.

Given my account of the duty to obey the law, obviously I appreciate the moral significance of fairness. I am not convinced that invoking it here will suffice, however, because voting is importantly different from other political chores for which one can be

---

4 What I explain in terms of fairness others might call "universality" or "universalizability."

plausibly required to do one's fair share. To see why, notice that if I fail to pay my taxes or fail to show up when summoned for jury duty, for instance, then I have not done my fair share and, as a result, others are left with more than their fair share of the *burden*. If I elect not to vote, on the other hand, no one else is unfairly burdened. Quite the contrary; if anything, those who do vote appear to be *benefited* by my abstinence because they are thereby left with more than their fair share of political influence. Thus, if we think of one's vote as the share of political influence to which one is entitled, failing to vote appears tantamount to merely giving greater political influence to one's compatriots, and it is hard to see what is objectionably unfair about that. If so, not only does it appear impossible to explain the duty to vote in terms of consequences, it is unclear how nonconsequential considerations like fairness will help.

This dismissal of fairness may be too quick, however, because even if one's vote can be thought of as one's fair share of political influence, there may be a way to explain why not voting places an unfair burden on one's compatriots. Specifically, if one thinks that a healthy democracy is a public good, then it seems plausible to insist that each of us has a duty to vote as her fair share of sustaining a healthy democracy. (Indeed, on this account, merely voting may not be enough; one might have a duty to cast an *adequately informed* ballot.)

The idea of a healthy democracy being a public good could be defended in two ways. According to the first, one could simply assert that, other things being equal, people in democracies are better off when citizens take the time to learn about and vote for the various candidates. A second, purely instrumental line of argument does not insist that there is anything intrinsically valuable about a healthy democracy; it relies on the empirical claim that healthy democracies tend to lead to more efficient, just, and beneficial governance. (Of course, one might claim that healthy democracies are a public good because they are both instrumentally and intrinsically valuable.) Assuming that at least one of these defenses is adequate, then we are all benefited by living in a healthy democracy and harmed (or at least not fully benefited) by living in an unhealthy democracy.[5] If so, then it seems reasonable to say that I am not merely waiving my right to exercise my share of political influence when I fail to vote; I am also failing to do my fair share to contribute to the public good of a healthy democracy. Thus, perhaps individuals in a democracy have a duty to vote, not because there would be any discernible consequences from one individual's failure to do so, but because there would be deleterious effects if an insufficient number of people took the time to act as responsible citizens.

The foregoing is the best way I know of to argue for a duty to vote, and I must confess that it could not reasonably be called a samaritan duty. To put the point bluntly, the United States does not strike me as a healthy democracy, but it would clearly be an abuse of ordinary language to say that those living in the United States are thereby imperiled.[6] If so, then we cannot say that the duty to perform easy rescues requires one to do one's part in promoting a healthy democracy. To summarize: While those who live in an unhealthy democracy may understandably *wish* that their compatriots were more responsible citizens, they do not need to be rescued, and thus there is no samaritan duty to be an active citizen *even if the demands of active citizenship are not unreasonably costly.*

Assuming that the "democracy as a public good" argument is both (1) the most compelling case for the duty to vote and (2) incompatible with samaritanism, we now face something of a crossroads. On the one hand, we might insist that because governments are ideally suited to secure the provision of public goods

---

5 Lomasky and Brennan contest this assumption in "Is There a Duty to Vote?" I will grant this premise here for the purposes of argument. As I will explain shortly, I think the argument can be successfully countered on other grounds.

6 One salient barometer of a democracy's health is voter turnout. In the United States, the participation rate is typically roughly 50 percent for presidential elections. Significantly fewer vote for so-called off-year elections. I should add that I do not deny that people are in fact imperiled in some unhealthy democracies; I deny only that the democracy's lack of health is the proximate cause of their peril. (Most people in healthy democracies are obviously not imperiled and, depending upon one's conception of democracy, some in a healthy democracy could be imperiled.)

and because a healthy democracy is a particularly important public good, there is nothing impermissible about states legally requiring their citizens to vote. On the other hand, we might concede that a healthy democracy is a public good but deny that it is important enough to justify the coercion necessary to secure it. According to this latter option, any law making it a crime not to vote would be unjust. This may be a matter about which reasonable people might disagree, but here I will argue for this second option.

I think it is impermissible to force people to do their fair share to sustain healthy democracies because, even if having a healthy democracy is a public good, it does not seem important enough to ground an enforceable duty. If we appropriately value individual self-determination, then we should permit nonconsensual coercion only if an agent is harming others or if this coercion is necessary to avert some especially grave evil. If one allowed nonconsensual coercion whenever it was necessary to promote some good at least as important as a healthy democracy, on the other hand, then one would open the door far too widely to coercion and give far too little deference to the importance of personal autonomy.

To appreciate the force of this point, think again of our hypothetical Mother Teresa. Specifically, imagine that Teresa would prefer not to take the time to learn about the various candidates running for public office (and she does not want to vote since she feels uncomfortable voting unless she knows a decent amount about the candidates) because she would rather spend that time ministering to those who are starving to death. Would it be permissible to criminally punish Teresa for tending to the infirm rather than doing her share to sustain a healthy democracy? I would suggest not. It seems to me that, even if we can rightly say that (1) a democracy will remain healthy only so long as a sufficient proportion of its constituents take the time to be good citizens, (2) a sufficient number of citizens will do their fair share only if legally required to do so, and (3) it would be an undeniably bad thing if a democracy becomes unhealthy, this is still not enough to justify forcing Teresa to turn her attention away from those starving to death and toward political matters because the latter are not sufficiently pressing. I do not think that those starving to death have a right that Teresa dedicate every waking moment to their plight, nor do I think that Teresa's compatriots have a right that she spend even a minimal amount of her time on political education and voting. Instead, I think that Teresa enjoys a morally privileged position of dominion over her own affairs that entitles her to decide how to spend her time on these or other matters.

Let me stress, however, that in denying a duty to vote, I am not supposing that no one can be subject to moral praise and blame for her level of political participation. My more modest claim is merely that this commendation and criticism are better conceived of in terms of virtue ethics than as juridical matters. Thus, I would describe our hypothetical Teresa as worthy of moral criticism for neglecting the responsibilities of citizenship even though she obviously merits moral applause for her extraordinary compassion. The crucial point for our purposes, though, is that no matter how morally deficient Teresa is in terms of her political participation, she violates no moral *duty* in failing to vote, and it would be no more permissible to punish her criminally than it would be to punish me criminally for failing to spend as much time and energy as Teresa does ministering to those starving to death. Teresa's compliance with the just laws of a legitimate regime is a juridical matter on which it is permissible to impose nonconsensual coercion, but it is impermissible to require someone to vote and it would be unjust to punish someone for failing to do so.

Moreover, it is worth noting that one need not have Mother Teresa's character and alternate uses of time in order to qualify for the right to personal autonomy. Each of us enjoys a privileged position of moral dominion over her own affairs, and thus everyone is normally entitled to decide which, if any, public goods to support. As a consequence, the government may not permissibly force me to do my share of supporting a healthy democracy even if, left to my own devices, I would spend the time I might be voting staring at my navel. Were this not the case, and were governments justified in forcing citizens to support every public good that was at least as important as a healthy democracy, then governments would be permitted to leave their constituents with no leisure time for art, literature, friendship, and such. I take this conclusion's absurdity to be self-evident.[7]

Given my accounts of political legitimacy and political obligation, clearly I do not think that an individual's moral right to self-determination is indefeasible. Because states are necessary to rescue us from the perils of the state of nature, they are justified in coercing us, and because they could not do so without sufficient numbers of us contributing to their efforts, we are obligated to obey the just laws of a legitimate regime. But just because I assert that states may sometimes coerce us, it does not follow that I would permit them to do so whenever they want or even whenever it is necessary to secure a public good. If a public good is insufficiently important, for instance, then its maintenance is not a weighty enough concern to justify coercing people. And because people do not seem horribly imperiled by their residence within relatively unhealthy democracies, I am not prepared to license governments to do all that they can to secure the health of their democracies. Thus, I am not ultimately worried by samaritanism's

---

7 A careful reader might be puzzled at this point by an asymmetry between my theory of the duty to obey the law and my account of virtuous citizenship. In particular, given that I single out political peril as distinctive, why do I not similarly single out all political public goods as special? Put in terms of my own example, if I insist that a state may permissibly force Mother Teresa to contribute her fair share to the elimination of political peril, why do I not also insist that the state may coerce Mother Teresa to be a good citizen? Does consistency not require me to assert that, although states ordinarily may not force their constituents to be virtuous, they are distinctly allowed to force virtuous citizenship?

I acknowledge that this asymmetry exists, but notice that it stems from my appreciation of personal autonomy, not from a mere inconsistency in reasoning. To see this, recall that I argue that political peril justifies coercion only because it involves two essential features: (1) sufficiently dire peril and (2) a coordination problem that can be solved only by the state. If either of these features were absent, then I would not defend statism. As a consequence, there is no inconsistency in my denying that states may permissibly force their constituents to be good citizens (even if securing a healthy democracy is a coordination problem that can be solved only by the state) because unhealthy democracies do not place people in sufficiently dire peril.

inability to explain the duty to vote because I conclude that any law legally requiring one to vote is unjust. None of this is intended to suggest that we should not be concerned about the troubling apathy exhibited by far too many citizens in existing democracies like the United States. But while we should clearly do more to educate and inspire people to be more virtuous citizens, it would be wrong to resort to laws like those in Australia and Belgium, which legally require people to vote.[8]

Military Service

Let us now consider the duty to serve in the military during times of national crisis. This duty presents a distinct type of challenge for defenders of the samaritan approach because, while military service might rescue one's compatriots from peril, it appears far too costly to count as merely a samaritan chore. This creates a substantial problem for the samaritan approach because most people take it for granted that an important responsibility of citizenship is being willing to serve when one's country most needs one. Many insist that forced military conscription, typically referred to as the "draft," should be utilized only in exceptional circumstances, but it is widely affirmed that there is nothing wrong with one's country calling one to serve during a time of need, and that one has a duty to serve when called upon to do so.

To begin, notice that there is a potential strategy for those who might want to allege that the draft is compatible with samaritanism. Specifically, if one both (1) insists that the draft may be utilized in only the most exceptional circumstances (when a country is faced with an attack that could not be successfully rebuffed with only those soldiers who would voluntarily agree to fight, for instance) and (2) emphasizes that the burdens of military service need to be balanced against all of the benefits that a

8 Let me add that, although I believe that a healthy democracy is a public good and that we have reason to work to make all democracies as healthy as possible, I mean to imply neither that only democratic governments are legitimate nor that one could not have an obligation to obey the laws of an undemocratic government.

typical citizen enjoys over the course of her life, then one might claim that the costs of military service should not be characterized as "unreasonably costly." Moreover, one might suggest that since not everyone will be called to serve (indeed, if the draft is instituted only under the highly restricted circumstances in which it is permissible, it is extremely unlikely that the average person will be tapped for service), the appropriate measure of costs is not thought of in terms of those actually serving, but instead takes account of the *chances* that one will have to serve. If so, then the relevant costs of the draft are *the costs to those who must serve divided by the total number of citizens.* Thus, once the costs are both measured in these terms and balanced against the benefits of citizenship over a lifetime, the government no longer need be regarded as imposing an unreasonable cost upon its citizens when it drafts a select few into military service only when necessary to secure the institutions that provide such important benefits for all of its constituents.

Although I do not think that the preceding analysis is outlandish – indeed, in many ways it squares well with the commonly held conviction that the benefits of citizenship generate a responsibility to pitch in during times of national crisis – I will not defend it here principally because I am wary of justifying the burdens and benefits of policies in terms of their effects upon the population as a whole. I think that we should not lose sight of the costs that any given law has for people considered individually, and thus I am suspicious of any analysis that implies that forcing an individual to fight in a war is not an enormous imposition upon that particular person. What is more, for the purposes of this discussion, I will not explore other, extrasamaritan ways to justify the draft even in circumstances of national emergency. Instead, for the purposes of argument, I shall presume that neither samaritanism nor any compatible value can explain the duty to serve in the military and then will argue that this does not constitute a reason to jettison the samaritan approach.

I do not think advocates of samaritan theory need be embarrassed by their apparent inability to justify the draft because I am not convinced that forced military service is permissible. I acknowledge that there may be times when countries are under attack and massive armies will be needed to defend the entire population, but I am not convinced that conscripting soldiers against their will is justified in even these extreme circumstances. I believe that individual self-determination remains important even in these extraordinary times, and thus I think that considerable efforts can and should be made to get people to enlist voluntarily in the armed services. What is more, I think that there are two ways in which this might be accomplished. First and most obviously, if a country is genuinely unable to defend itself with its existing troops (which I assume is among the prerequisites for a permissible draft), then there is reason to suppose that hoards of people would voluntarily sign up to defend their homeland. Of course, the threat in question might be too remote or too overpowering, and thus people either could not be convinced that the country needs their services or could be afraid to enlist because doing so would appear tantamount to suicide. Such conditions admittedly might deter people from voluntarily serving, but they could equally cause problems for justifying the draft because it would be curious if a threat were imminent enough to justify forcing people to fight but simultaneously appeared so remote that average citizens were not inspired to fight it. It is equally problematic to suggest that a threat could be so overwhelming that normal people would regard fighting it as a nearly certain death sentence and yet the government would not be asking too much of its citizens to force them to take on this mission. (Whatever one thinks of kamikaze fighters or suicide bombers, it seems clear that a government should never force someone into such a role.)

Secondly, even if we could somehow imagine a hypothetical scenario in which a threat was sufficiently imminent but not too overpowering, and yet people would not freely sign up to resist it, this would not be enough to justify the draft because there would be other, less coercive ways to mobilize the necessary troops. Given that coerced military service is problematic both because it is nonconsensual and because it heaps a disproportionate share of costs upon the few soldiers conscripted, a preferable way to

handle these extraordinary circumstances might be to raise soldiers' salaries (dramatically, if need be) until a sufficient number
of citizens were willing to sign up for a tour of military duty. Assuming that those who enlist are not actively misled about the
dangers involved, this proposal has the potential both to spread
the costs more evenly among all citizens and to eliminate forced
conscription of soldiers. And, again, if there was a circumstance
in which the threat was not grave enough to motivate the population to pay the higher taxes necessary to pay the increased
wages, then it is hard to see how this threat could be sufficient to
justify forced conscription.

Here, one might object that, insofar as the least advantaged
would be most susceptible to being financially lured into the military, my proposal would in the end be tantamount to drafting
the poor by another name. The concern is that offering markedly
higher wages would be insufficient to entice the relatively well
off, and thus the poor would be stuck doing the risky work of
protecting the state. In fact, one might even think that my plan
is *worse* than a draft by random lottery because it would in practice exacerbate a society's class divisions by further burdening the
least well off with the horrible task of fighting the most dangerous
wars.

I acknowledge that the least advantaged would likely be disproportionately inclined to sign up for military service at increased
wages, but I deny that this necessarily renders my proposal unjust, and I certainly do not think my suggestion should be characterized as merely drafting the poor by another name. First of
all, notice that many existing armies are disproportionately populated by men and women from the lower socioeconomic classes
who regard the military as their best career option, and yet few
would suggest that these people are being effectively forced to
serve. And with good reason. Certainly it is unfortunate that some
people have fewer opportunities for rewarding careers, but it is
equally certainly a mistake to describe all but the relatively well
off as "forced" to take their jobs. Depending upon the level of
economic pressure involved, there may or may not be something
unjust about people who feel that they have no viable alternative

to fighting in a risky war, but there is a very real and important distinction between almost all kinds of financial pressure and legal coercion backed by criminal punishment.

Second, even if there were a situation in which people's economic circumstances were so dire that it was scarcely an exaggeration to say that they were forced to enlist in a dangerous military campaign, the injustice would be located in the prevailing economic conditions that leave these people imperiled.[9] In other words, if increased wages for risky military service are unjust in these circumstances, it is because of the harsh economic context, not the offer itself. In these conditions, the injustice is present whether or not the military wages are offered; the latter merely call attention to the preexisting injustice. Moreover, while I have some sympathy for the more nuanced criticism that offering increased wages for harmful work exacerbates the injustice already present, even this more modest claim is problematic because it seems as though the worrisome element in this case would be offering the work at all. That is, it is hard to believe that what makes the offer bad is that the government is offering *increased* compensation. Finally, even if this objection were compelling, it would not show that offering increased wages to fight in wars is always wrong; at most, it would show that we should be wary of doing so *in cases where there is extreme and oppressive poverty.*

In a different vein, one might protest that offering higher wages in no way solves the problem of nonvoluntary coercion because these wages could not be raised without increasing taxes that are themselves coercive. According to an objector of this stripe, my proposed "solution" is in one important respect actually worse because it involves wrongly coercing all taxpayers, not merely the few military conscripts necessary to fight the war.

I am in part receptive to this criticism because I agree that not all taxation is justified and that, even when well intentioned,

---

9 For a samaritan-oriented analysis of the conditions under which coercion and/or exploitation is impermissible, please see Chapter V of my *A Theory of Secession: The Case for Political Self-Determination* (Cambridge: Cambridge University Press, 2005).

wrongful taxation is merely institutionally licensed theft. Nevertheless, I do not find this objection compelling because even substantial taxation need not be unjustified, and it strikes me that if taxation could ever be permissible, it would be when necessary to fund a war of self-defense. Of course, there may be circumstances in which a government either exaggerates the threat in question or raises taxes more than is necessary to avert this threat, but obviously nothing about my proposal requires me to defend such state practices. Most importantly, though, I resist the implicit premise that any proposal that coerces more people is automatically worse than one that coerces fewer. Certainly it would be better to coerce fewer people when one holds everything else constant, but the options we are considering emphatically do not do this. Rather, my proposal coerces more people only so that it can substitute a minimal and equitable level of coercion on everyone for an unreasonable and inequitable amount of coercion on a randomly selected few. And because each of us is equally bound to do her fair share of samaritan chores, I consider it a decided advantage of my proposal that it spreads the coercion more thinly and equitably, even if it spreads it more widely.

Finally, I should acknowledge that I can imagine a scenario in which one would have a moral duty to fight in a war and where others may have a right to force you to do so. Suppose, for instance, that some evil empire was attacking an innocent country, and, if victorious, the Evils would rape, kill, and/or enslave many of the Innocents. Imagine also that the balance of power was such that, if you failed to fight on behalf of the Innocents, the Evils would very likely prevail, but if you did lend your efforts to the fight, the Innocents would defeat the Evils. In circumstances like these, it seems to me that you might have a duty to fight for the Innocents, and the Innocents could be justified in forcing you to do so if this were the only way to get you to join the fight. For several reasons, however, this concession does not open the door to anything like traditional military drafts. First and most obviously, this hypothetical scenario is exceptionally unlikely to occur in the real world. (As I outlined earlier, it is hard to imagine that people would have to be coerced to fight in these circumstances, especially if military wages were dramatically increased.) Second, notice that this scenario says nothing about your sex or age. The point, of course, is that if a draft were necessary, there is no reason to assume that it must be restricted to males between the ages of eighteen and twenty-six, for instance. Third and most importantly, notice also that this scenario makes no mention of whether you are a citizen of the innocent country. As I see it, if there is a duty to fight on behalf of the Innocents in these circumstances, it does not depend upon being a fellow citizen of the Innocents; one could equally be bound if one were a citizen of some neutral neighboring country or even if one were a citizen of the aggressive, evil country. My point is that, in the extraordinary circumstances in which one had a duty to fight in a war, it would not be a distinctively *political* duty owed to one's country and/or compatriots. Rather, this duty would be triggered by samaritan considerations that could be owed to fellow human beings across political borders as long as they were sufficiently imperiled and could be saved only by your not unreasonably costly efforts.

In sum, then, I am inclined to concede that samaritanism does not have the resources to justify extremely costly political sacrifices like the traditional uses of military conscription. I am unfazed by this implication, however, because I am not convinced that it is permissible for a government to force its constituents to serve in the military even under extreme circumstances where the country must assemble a large army to defend itself against a dangerous and aggressive threat.

Conclusion

I have argued that there is neither a duty to vote nor a duty to serve in one's country's military, even in times of national crisis. Without retracting either of these conclusions, let me reiterate that my chief goal in this chapter is to support a more general thesis. I focus on voting and military service in order to defend the samaritan account of our duty to obey the law against the charge that it cannot justify all of the political obligations commonly thought to exist.

Although some might try to stretch and bend samaritanism so that it justifies much more than one would initially suspect, I have pursued a different strategy here. This strategy involves emphasizing two things. First, if there are various functions that governments legitimately perform, presumably we can tell a compelling story that explains why states are right to take on these tasks. Many of these stories may invoke values other than samaritanism, but there is no reason to suppose that a defender of the samaritan approach must insist that samaritan values are the only ones that matter. My argument that samaritanism and fairness are the core normative premises in a satisfactory theory of our duty to obey the law does not commit me to the view that these are the *only* values relevant to political theory. Accordingly, we must not assume that an advocate of samaritanism cannot agree that states are right to perform various chores necessary to achieve other goals like effective democratic governance and freedom from oppression.[10]

Second and more importantly, we need not accept at face value every political duty pretheoretically thought to exist. Indeed, if there is one core lesson to be taken from this chapter, it is that it is a strenth rather than a drawback of the samaritan approach that it begins with a minimal state and then insists that additional political functions may be justified only with a compelling explanation of why these functions are both sufficiently important and unavailable if not supplied by the state. Thus, if the preceding discussions of the duties to vote and serve in the military are instructive, it is because they suggest that a pair of widely accepted political duties may not be genuine after all. If someone more imaginative than I could construct a decisive argument in defense of either duty, this would not refute the samaritan theory (though, it would be worrisome if this argument were incompatible with espousing samaritan values) because the general lesson

---

10 By securing effective democratic governance, I mean (among other things) securing people's right to vote. This is not inconsistent with my argument about the duty to vote because the *right* to vote often should be protected even if there is no enforceable *duty* to do so.

would remain: We should not assume without argument that everything existing states do is legitimate, nor should we presume that every moral duty that states have historically listed as a component of responsible citizenship is genuine.

To emphasize: I am an unapologetic statist because I think that states are necessary to provide extremely important benefits that could not be secured in their absence. But just because we need states to do some things, it does not follow that they should be permitted to do anything that they can or even everything that they can do well. For each potential state function, we should ask whether the goods secured are important enough to justify the nonconsensual coercion that inevitably accompanies political coordination. And even if the function is important enough, we must be sure that noncoercive, extragovernmental means could not satisfactorily secure the benefits. To put this point in terms of a rather banal example, it is not clear why states must be in the business of delivering the mail. There may have been a time when securing safe postal communication was sufficiently important and could only have been accomplished by states, but even if so, that time has almost certainly passed. In a day with phones, e-mail, faxes, and highly reliable private couriers, it seems clear that governmental postal carriers are not providing a crucial service that would necessarily be unavailable in their absence. I consider this case banal because constituents are typically coerced neither to use nor to subsidize the state's postal service. (No one is legally forced to send mail, and people are free to use private couriers if they choose.) But in most cases, the forced imposition of any nonessential state function is not only inefficient, it is unjust. (A country's military buildup is far less benign, for instance, both because citizens are taxed to pay for it and because countries with great military capabilities are prone to use them to ill effect.) What we should do in the face of these unjust laws is not an easy question, but it is the question to which we shall now turn.

4　Confronting Injustice

E VEN if there is a general moral duty to obey the just laws of a legitimate regime, it remains an open question how one should respond when confronted with either an unjust law or an illegitimate regime. The answer to this question will in many cases be quite complicated. At a minimum, though, I contend that there is a general obligation to obey neither unjust laws nor any law of an illegitimate regime. More ambitiously, I submit that there are potentially weighty moral reasons to actively resist unjust laws and illegitimate regimes.

Illegitimate Regimes

In developing my argument for the duty to obey the law, I have been assuming throughout that the laws in particular were just and that the regimes in general were legitimate. In this section, I want to explore whether we are similarly obligated to obey the legal commands of an illegitimate regime. I will advance a number of theses, but the two most basic are that (1) there is no general duty to comply with the laws of an illegitimate regime, and (2) there are actually moral reasons to resist illegitimate governments.

Here I will restrict my discussion to two countries: Iraq under Saddam Hussein, which I will assume was an illegitimate military dictatorship, and apartheid South Africa, which I understand to have been an illegitimate regime that wrongly oppressed blacks. Moreover, unless I specify otherwise, when I speak of a law in this section, I mean to refer to a just law or, if one prefers, a law that *would be* just if it were imposed by a legitimate regime. I make this simplifying assumption so as not to confuse the issues of a regime's illegitimacy with a particular law's injustice.

First, consider whether the average citizen would have a general duty to obey the law in Saddam Hussein's Iraq. At first glance, one might think that the answer must be "Yes." After all, despite its atrocious record on human rights, this regime was able to secure a stable peace, thereby eliminating many of the perils of the state of nature. This response would be too quick, however, because it fails to appreciate the exorbitant costs attached to being a citizen in such a country. One can explain this point in terms of the analogy invoked earlier of Beth commandeering Cathy's car in order to rush Amy to the hospital. Specifically, while Beth might be justified in *borrowing* Cathy's car in these extreme circumstances, Beth may not *steal* Cathy's car even if she subsequently uses it, among other purposes, to take Beth to the hospital. The reason for this is straightforward: Although Beth needs to use Cathy's car in order to save Amy, she does not need to keep it permanently. And because Beth is permitted at most to do those things necessary to complete her samaritan mission, she cannot invoke Amy's peril to justify stealing the car. Of course, the analogous reasoning applies to Cathy's obligations. Because having one's car stolen is unnecessary to save Amy, Cathy would have no duty to surrender her keys to a thief like Beth.

Insofar as Hussein's government placed so many unnecessary costs upon its citizens, I think its imposition was analogous to Beth's stealing rather than borrowing Cathy's car. If so, the analogy can help us identify at least three explanations for why those subject to Hussein's government had no obligation to obey its laws. First, according to the theory advanced here, one's duty to obey the law is conceived as a samaritan chore. If a government exploits its citizens for the rulers' personal gain, however, then it is designed to transform the constituents' burdens into benefits for the elite rulers. As such, it places unreasonable costs on its subjects, and thus obeying the law cannot qualify as a samaritan chore. A second and related explanation of the absence of the duty to obey the law can be given in terms of fairness. Because the duty to obey the law is understood as one's *fair share* of a communal samaritan project, it seems clear that the profound unfairness of Iraq's laws would have undermined any chance that they might have obligated those they constrained. Since the legal institutions were designed to unfairly profit Hussein and his cronies, it is no surprise that a view featuring fairness would not require one to support such an unjust distribution of burdens and benefits. Third and perhaps most important, regardless of the specifics of one's favored account of the duty to obey the law, it would be awkward to suppose that one can be obligated to support one's own oppression. One would be loath to suggest that a slave could have a duty to support the institution of slavery, for instance. This is relevant to our discussion here, of course, because Hussein's regime oppressed its constituents in something like the way that slavery oppresses slaves. If so, then one could not affirm an Iraqi's obligation to obey the law unless one were willing to accept that people may be morally required to do their part to support those institutions that enslave or otherwise brutally oppress them. For a variety of compelling reasons, then, it seems clear that there is no general duty to obey the law in oppressive military dictatorships like Saddam Hussein's Iraq.

Let us turn now to apartheid South Africa. I presume that it is obvious that the blacks in this country had no general duty to obey the law for the same reasons that Iraqis had no such duty: Legal obedience would have been unreasonably costly, unfair, and tantamount to contributing to their own oppression. It is less obvious, however, whether the average white citizen should have obeyed the law. After all, the demands of citizenship were not unreasonably costly or unfair to the whites, nor did the legal institutions oppress white citizens any more than slavery oppresses the slave owners. In view of this, one might conclude that while the blacks had no duty to obey the law in apartheid South Africa, the whites did. This line of thinking should be rejected, however, because it underestimates the significance of supporting an institution that oppresses others. In particular, while it is true that obeying the law was not too costly for the whites, legal obedience in such a case was not merely doing one's part to support institutions that eliminated the perils of the state of nature. When the same legal system that secured political stability was also used to oppress blacks, obeying the law involved playing a part in perpetuating injustice. And since one cannot have a duty to support this type of horrible oppression, the whites cannot have had a duty to obey the laws of a country like apartheid South Africa.

It is worth emphasizing that this account of the whites' lack of obligation does not require one to deny that the South African government, by securing a stable political environment, supplied extremely important benefits. Reflecting on the obligation to keep promises might help illustrate this important point. It is widely believed that, although there is a general duty to keep promises, this does not apply to a promise to do something unjust. If Amber promises Betty that she will murder Carol, for instance, few think that Amber would actually have such a duty; instead, it is standard to presume that the injustice of murdering renders Amber's promise invalid. The crucial thing to note for our purposes is that, because promises to commit an injustice do not bind, it is not necessary to deny that Amber made such a promise. I think that we should reason along the same lines about the possibility of there being a duty to obey the laws of an unjust regime. That is, we do not need to deny that these legal institutions supply important benefits because we can assert that the injustice of the system renders invalid what would otherwise be a moral duty. Thus, just as Amber's promise cannot be binding when it requires her to perform an injustice, a legal regime's benefits cannot bind its constituents when legal obedience would involve supporting oppression. If this is right, then denying that there is a duty to support beneficial but unjust governments is no more problematic than denying that there is a duty to keep promises to perform unjust actions.

Expanding upon this last point, not only did citizens of countries like Iraq and apartheid South Africa have no duty to obey the law, it seems more plausible to posit the existence of moral reasons to *resist* such illegitimate regimes. Indeed, the idea here is essentially that which I stressed in Chapter 1 when criticizing philosophical anarchists for failing to own up to the radical implications of their views. There I suggested that, to be consistent, philosophical anarchists should not only deny the duty to obey the law, they should acknowledge the presumption in favor of opposing the government. My argument was that, given the voluntarist's aversion to nonconsensual coercion, she would seem committed to insisting that all of us have moral reasons to help eliminate such coercion. Philosophical anarchists like Simmons may be right to protest that there is no *general and absolute duty* to fight governments in every possible instance, but this does not undermine the more modest thesis that there are always *moral reasons* to oppose governments. What I am suggesting here is that the same reasoning applies in the case of illegitimate regimes. Not only did the oppression of states like Iraq and South Africa explain why their subjects had no general duty to obey their laws, it gave their constituents moral reasons to undermine the government's authority and thus to help eliminate the oppression. These moral reasons do not necessarily translate into a general and absolute duty to resist the illegitimate governments in all instances (among other things, resistance in certain circumstances might be too costly to be demanded by duty), but they always provide a moral presumption in favor of doing so. In short, just as the reasoning motivating philosophical anarchism implies that we have reason to subvert *all states*, the premises supporting my account of political legitimacy imply that we had reason to resist *illegitimate states* like Saddam Hussein's Iraq and apartheid South Africa.

Things are more complicated than they might at this point appear, however, because the reasons *against* obeying the laws of an illegitimate regime must be put on the scales with various moral reasons that may exist *in favor of* obeying any given law. As a consequence, it might be that a citizen should act as the law directs in some situations *even though the commands come from an illegitimate regime*. In other words, the reasons to resist illegitimate states are always potentially defeasible, and citizens are responsible for determining on a case-by-case basis whether they are in fact defeated. (Indeed, this is the wisdom in Simmons's assessment that

"The practical stance with respect to the state...should be one of careful consideration and thoughtful weighing of all of the reasons that bear on action in a particular set of political circumstances. The illegitimacy of a state...is just one moral factor among many bearing on how persons in that state should (or are permitted to) act."[1])

Having established that (1) there is no general duty to obey the laws of illegitimate regimes, (2) there are moral reasons to resist illegitimate states, and (3) the moral reasons to oppose illegitimate regimes are defeasible and thus must be weighed against countervailing considerations on a case-by-case basis, we now see how complex the moral matters of legal obedience can be for conscientious constituents of illegitimate states. Because I could not construct a better analogy to clarify such a complicated set of factors, let me instead quote at length from Chaim Gans.

> Picture a team of surgeons who share a single scalpel, and a gang of robbers who share a single switchblade. We clearly have a general obligation to preserve the scalpel and no such general obligation to preserve the switchblade. Suppose, though, that the robbers use the switchblade for other purposes besides robbery. Suppose they use it to combat a rival gang that specializes in murder. This fact may give rise to a general duty not to harm the switchblade. So far so good as to our general duties to the scalpel and the switchblade. These must be carefully distinguished, though, from the decisions which we should make about particular references to these instruments. Such decisions may be *affected* by the existence or non-existence of general duties, but they are not *dictated* by these duties. If a member of the surgery team tries to use the scalpel to slit open a personal letter addressed to one of his colleagues, this certainly isn't reason enough to damage the scalpel. The general duty to preserve the scalpel, a duty which we have acknowledged, overrides the value damaged by the scalpel's presently intended use, that is, the value of privacy. However, if one of the team members attempts murder with the scalpel, and the only means of prevention is damaging the scalpel, then there is then undoubtedly very good reason to do so. This damage will

1 Simmons, *Justification and Legitimacy*, p. 109.

not be caused because of the absence of duty to preserve the scalpel. It will be caused because this duty is overridden under the present circumstances by the value to be damaged through the scalpel's specific imminent use. Now, back to the bandits. Though there may be no reason to preserve their knife, this doesn't mean that there is no reason to preserve those goods produced by it that are not immoral. If, besides being used for robbery, the switchblade was also used to prepare food, the fact that it need not be preserved doesn't mean that the food need not be preserved. This last point may be likened to the matter of the good laws produced by a corrupt legal system.[2]

Gans's analogy is quite helpful because it reminds us that legal regimes and the particular laws of which they are comprised are powerful instruments and, as such, can be used for good and evil. Moreover, merely because a law is part of a corrupt regime, it does not follow that this particular law is useless or that the evil of the regime necessarily trumps the utility of the law. As Gans and Simmons both point out, there is no reason to rule out in advance that the importance of acting in accordance with a particular law can in some cases outweigh one's reasons to resist a generally illegitimate regime. Finally, as much as we might like one, there appears to be no simple algorithm capable of generating an exhaustive list of the conditions in which the importance of a particular just law takes precedence over the injustice of the system as a whole, and vice versa. In many instances, those governed by corrupt institutions must rely upon their moral sensibilities as they weigh competing moral considerations on a case-by-case basis.

One might despair because the arguments in this section are so complicated and fail ultimately to arrive at a simpler conclusion, but it seems to me that the morality of legal obedience in illegitimate regimes is an irredeemably complex matter, and any theory that glosses over the complexities would miss much of moral importance. Nonetheless, there are two basic points that can safely be extracted from this difficult section: (1) there is no general duty to obey the laws of an illegitimate regime, and (2)

2 Chaim Gans, *Philosophical Anarchism and Political Obedience* (Cambridge: Cambridge University Press, 1992), 107–8.

there are general moral reasons to disobey the laws of illegitimate states.

Unjust Laws

Let us now explore how a citizen of a legitimate state should respond when confronted with an unjust law. I am afraid that the moral reasoning here is no less complex than for someone facing a just law in an illegitimate regime. The good news, however, is that these two matters are in a sense mirror images of one another, so the work we have just done has helped to clear the path for our present inquiry. I will once again advance a number of subsidiary claims, but the basic theses I hope to defend in this section are that (1) there is no general duty to obey an unjust law of a legitimate regime, and (2) there are actually moral reasons to disobey these unjustified legal commands.

In pursuing this question, I will presume that Australia's government qualifies as a legitimate regime. Thus, following my analysis of the duty to vote, I will take Australia's legal requirement of voting as my example of an unjust law imposed by a legitimate regime. Given that the costs of voting are typically minimal and Australia's penalty of $50 is not terribly harsh, this is not an example of an utterly wicked and oppressive law. In some ways this is helpful, though, since it makes it easier to see how a particular unjust law need not by itself render the entire system illegitimate. The question I would like to address, then, is whether Australians have a duty to obey the law requiring them to vote, even though this law is unjust.

It is tempting to answer this question in the affirmative. After all, as a legitimate regime, the Australian government performs extremely valuable functions without making unreasonable demands on its citizens, so taking part in democratic elections hardly seems too much to ask. I would urge us to resist this conclusion, though. In my view, it is important to bear in mind that a government's mandate to perform certain crucial functions does not give it a blank check to treat its constituents however it chooses. The distinction between just and unjust laws is an important one, and there is nothing about affirming a citizen's duty to obey the former that prohibits one from denying a citizen's obligation to comply with the latter. To appreciate the force of this point, let us once again revisit the analogy of Beth commandeering Cathy's car in order to rush Amy to the hospital. Here I want to emphasize that one's conviction that Beth is justified in borrowing Cathy's car in no way commits one to the view that Beth can also take one of Cathy's compact discs out of the car when she has completed her run to the hospital. Even if it is true both that Beth has performed an extremely valuable service in saving Amy's life and that the loss of one compact disc is fairly insignificant in comparison to Amy's life, neither fact in any way entitles Beth to Cathy's compact disc. The essential point is that, even if Beth has a right to certain things necessary to saving Amy's life, she is entitled to *only* those things necessary to do so. As a consequence, it seems entirely appropriate to insist that, while Cathy has a moral duty to loan Beth her car, she has no duty to surrender any of the compact discs therein.

I hope this analogy makes the corresponding conclusions in the political realm more apparent. Even if the Australian government is entitled to impose itself upon its citizens in various ways in order to perform a number of extremely important functions, it is entitled to impose itself in only those ways necessary to do so. And if I was right to conclude in the previous chapter that sustaining a healthy democracy is not important enough to justify nonconsensual coercion, then there is nothing problematic about defending an obligation to obey just Australian laws while at the same time denying any duty to obey an unjust law like that which legally requires citizens to vote. For this reason, I deny that there is a general duty to obey the unjust laws of a legitimate regime.

Notice that not only is there no general duty to obey unjust laws, there are moral reasons to resist them. This is true of unjust laws for the same reasons we canvassed in connection with illegitimate regimes: It is not only possible in theory to distinguish between just and unjust laws, it is important in practice to empower a legitimate state to impose the former and to deter a government from imposing the latter. The reasoning in both cases is straightforward. The moral reasons all of us have to promote justice should move us to support those institutions that make the world more just and to resist those that make it less just. Because unjust laws make the world less just, clearly we have moral reasons to oppose them.

Matters are more complicated still, however, because disobeying a given law not only undermines that particular law, it also undercuts the authority of the entire system of which that law is a part. This provides no cause for concern when one is disobeying an unjust law imposed by an illegitimate regime, but it does raise issues if one is contesting an unjust law in a legitimate regime, like the Australian government's requirement that all citizens vote. In particular, while one should be pleased that one's disobedience is playing a part in weakening the state's capacity to require citizens to vote, one might be worried that one's disobedience is also thereby undermining the Australian government's standing as a whole. This latter effect is worrisome, of course, because legitimate states are precisely the types of institutions that one has moral reasons to support. One therefore typically has conflicting moral reasons when faced with an unjust law in a legitimate regime because (dis)obedience in such cases simultaneously affects both the bad capacities of the unjust law and the good capacities of the system as a whole. Thus, just as constituents in an illegitimate regime confront a difficult situation when faced with a just law, citizens of a legitimate regime must weigh competing reasons when confronted with an unjust legal command. In the latter case, the moral reasons generated by the legitimacy of the regime should motivate one to obey the law, and those reasons stemming from the injustice of the particular law should move one to disobey the law.

Once again, there appears to be no simple algorithm to help one adjudicate all such conflicts in advance. Instead, like someone struggling to decide whether to obey a just law in an illegitimate regime, the best that a citizen of a legitimate state can do when faced with an unjust law is to conscientiously weigh the competing considerations and act upon those that appear most stringent. It may not always be obvious in which direction the balance of reasons points, but perhaps we can at least get a helpful glimpse of the process by considering how an Australian citizen should react to the legal duty to vote. On the one hand, the injustice of the law requiring citizens to vote should be opposed; thus, one might be inclined to stay away from the polls in order to do one's share of a larger effort to undermine that particular law's authority. On the other hand, there are several reasons to resist this conclusion. First and most obviously, the legitimacy of the Australian government gives one moral reasons to refrain from acting in ways that will undermine its capacity to perform its requisite functions. Secondly, compared with other unjust laws, the legal requirement to vote is a relatively benign one because it both requires relatively little of its citizens and is designed to promote a good cause (promoting healthy democracy is much better than fostering racism, for instance). Third and finally, it is important to bear in mind that virtuous citizens would vote; thus, whatever reasons one has to be a virtuous citizen happen to weigh against breaking this particular law. As a result, I am inclined to conclude that, while in this instance there is neither a duty to vote nor a duty to disobey the law requiring one to vote, the balance of moral reasons favors voting. Let me add, however, that perhaps the most virtuous citizen would not only vote but work via various other channels to get the government to repeal its unjust law requiring people to vote.

I regret that this analysis of a citizen's moral responsibilities in the face of unjust laws is just as complicated as the preceding discussion of illegitimate regimes. Once again, though, we are in a position to close by underscoring two basic claims: (1) there is no general duty to obey the unjust laws of a legitimate state, and (2) there are general moral reasons to disobey unjust laws.

Civil Disobedience

Before concluding, I would like to comment briefly on a citizen's responsibility to either practice or abstain from civil disobedience. Many people list various conditions that must be satisfied in order for civil disobedience to be permissible (e.g., that it be principled, public, and nonviolent). I agree that these conditions are often illuminating, but I deny that they are normally required to justify its practice. On the contrary; I think civil disobedience quite often is easily justified and that the conditions theorists typically list are better thought of as ideals to approximate if one seeks to have one's message received in the most sympathetic and effective light. In fact, I would suggest that civil disobedience is not only easy to justify, it is also seldom obligatory because it is in many cases too costly to the civilly disobedient. Often the civilly disobedient are to be applauded as virtuous citizens, and the only reason people writing on this topic have not always appreciated this is that they have been overly impressed with the authority of law, even the unjust laws of illegitimate regimes. To see this, notice how people responded to Martin Luther King, Jr.'s campaign of civil disobedience.

Many condemned King, even while acknowledging that his ends were laudable, simply because he advocated deliberately breaking the law. Louis Waldman, for instance, argued as follows:

> Those who assert rights under the Constitution and the laws made thereunder must abide by that Constitution and the law, if that Constitution is to survive. They cannot pick and choose; they cannot say they will abide by those laws which they think are just and refuse to abide by those laws which they think are unjust....
>
>   The country, therefore, cannot accept Dr. King's doctrine that he and his followers will pick and choose, knowing that it is illegal to do so. I say, such doctrine is not only illegal and for that reason alone should be abandoned, but that it is also immoral, destructive of the principles of democratic government, and a danger to the very civil rights Dr. King seeks to promote.[3]

In short, King should be criticized because it is always and in every case impermissible to deliberately break the law.

3 Louis Waldman, "Civil Rights – Yes: Civil Disobedience – No (A Reply to Dr. Martin Luther King)," in Hugo Adam Bedau (ed.), *Civil Disobedience: Theory and Practice* (New York: Pegasus Books, 1967), 106 and 107. Quoted in James Rachels, *The Elements of Moral Philosophy* (Boston: McGraw-Hill, 1999), p. 156.

A less severe position adopts a more permissive stance with respect to civil disobedience as long as it satisfies various conditions. As one might expect, there is no consensus regarding which particular conditions must be satisfied, but it has been common to suggest that the disobedience must be (1) principled, (2) public, (3), nonviolent, (4) expected to be efficacious, (5) resorted to only after sufficient attempts to reform via legal means have proved ineffective, and (6) engaged in by only those willing to accept the legal punishment for breaking the law. According to some, then, King's civil disobedience was morally permissible only because he broke the law for principled reasons rather than for personal gain; he did so in a public rather than a clandestine fashion; he never resorted to violence against either the authorities or innocent third parties; he reasonably expected his disobedience to be an effective catalyst for legal reforms; he pursued legal avenues before advocating civil disobedience; and he did not try to escape criminal prosecution and punishment.

I agree that King should not be criticized for breaking the law, but I deny that his behavior was permissible only because it satisfied some subset of the preceding conditions. On my view, King was morally at liberty to break the particular laws he disobeyed simply because they were unjust. Moreover, not only did King have no duty to obey these particular laws, he actually had moral reasons to oppose them. I would not go so far as to say that he had a duty to break these laws (and certainly he had no obligation to break them in the exemplary fashion that he did), however, because it is asking too much to demand that someone suffer the consequences that typically attend such disobedience. As I see it, King was an exemplary citizen because he did not merely disobey the laws, he worked hard and sacrificed mightily so that these laws would be reformed and the government as a whole would become more just. Any conscientious person would be troubled by the unjust and inequitable laws against which King fought, but only an extraordinarily virtuous citizen would dedicate his life to reforming the corrupt legal institutions in King's selfless fashion. Indeed, King's virtue seems so striking as to be self-evident to all those who do not overestimate the authority of law. Once one distinguishes between just and unjust laws and recognizes our reasons to support the former and resist the latter, it is hard to imagine someone failing to recognize King's particular form of lawbreaking as the exemplary behavior it is.

Conclusion

Given that legitimate and illegitimate regimes can each have just and unjust laws, a citizen may be faced with four possibilities: (1) a just law imposed by an illegitimate regime, (2) an unjust law imposed by a legitimate regime, (3) an unjust law imposed by an illegitimate regime, and (4) a just law imposed by a legitimate regime. This chapter has analyzed the first two possibilities and concluded that there is a general duty to obey neither unjust laws nor the laws of an illegitimate regime. In addition, I have argued that a subject confronted with a just law in an illegitimate regime must weigh the reasons in favor of obeying this particular law against the moral reasons to subvert the regime in general. Similarly, I have suggested that a citizen facing an unjust law in a legitimate state must weigh the moral reasons to support the legitimate regime against the specific reasons to oppose this particular law.

The third and fourth possibilities are much less complex. Obviously, there is no general duty to obey an unjust law imposed by an illegitimate regime. In this case, the injustice of the law and the illegitimacy of the regime both provide reasons against legal obedience. Finally, nothing about the analysis in this chapter in any way undermines my core thesis that there is a general duty to obey the just laws of a legitimate regime. It is important to acknowledge, though, that things are not necessarily always simple even for a citizen facing a just law in a legitimate regime because, though *general*, the duty to obey such laws is clearly not *absolute*. In other words, although a citizen invariably has a duty to obey the just laws of a legitimate regime, this duty is liable to be overridden by a sufficiently urgent competing consideration.

When faced with a choice between either disrespecting her brother, Polynices, or disobeying a law prohibiting her from burying him, Sophocles' Antigone ultimately felt compelled to break the law. Similarly, E. M. Forster famously reflected: "If I had to choose between betraying my country and betraying my friend, I hope that I should have the guts to betray my country." Whatever one believes about the justness of the law Antigone faced, about whether she acted rightly, or about whether Forster would be right to betray his country in the name of friendship, the more general point remains: Surely there are some circumstances in which one's duty to obey the law could be overridden by a more stringent duty.[4]

My recognition that the duty to obey the law is not absolute in no way constitutes a retreat from my earlier thesis because the assertion that there is a *general* duty to obey the law does not commit one to the further, implausible claim that this duty is always and in every case *decisive*. Why think that the general duty to obey the law must be absolute when we do not suppose that this must be the case for other general duties, like the duty to keep one's promises? Indeed, given that virtually everyone appreciates that the general duty to fulfill one's valid promises can be overridden, it would be curious if anyone thought the duty to obey the law must be absolute. So, while one might regret that the moral path is not always simple and straightforward even for a citizen faced with a law whose content and pedigree are both unimpeachable, my conclusion remains intact: Just as valid promises create

---

4 Notice that it is not even true that the general duty to obey the just laws of a legitimate regime can be overridden only by a more stringent duty. As Frances Kamm has argued in her essay "Supererogation and Obligation" (*Journal of Philosophy* 82[3] [1985]: 118–38), for instance, there are cases in which one may permissibly ignore a duty in order to do something supererogatory. Although Donna's promise to meet Carol for lunch clearly gives her a duty to do so, for example, surely Donna would act rightly if she missed the date in order to rescue imperiled infants from a burning house that she came across on her way to meeting Carol. By the same token, presumably Donna would do no wrong if she broke the law against jaywalking as she ran across the street and into the burning house.

a general duty to act as promised, just laws in legitimate regimes create a general duty to act as the laws command.

Let me conclude by answering the question at hand: "Is there a duty to obey the law?" Yes, each of us is obligated to obey the just laws of a legitimate regime as her fair share of the communal samaritan chore of rescuing all of us from the perils of the state of nature.

II The Duty to Obey and Our Natural Moral Duties

A. John Simmons

5   The Problem and Its Significance

I N one sense, of course, there is a very easy answer to the question "Is there a duty to obey the law?" Imposing duties is an important part of what the law is *for*. Legal systems, especially in their criminal law components, specify the duties of those who fall within the relevant jurisdictions, typically backing those assignments of duty with the threat of legal sanction for nonperformance. So, of course, there is (at least normally) a duty to obey the law. But the duty at issue in this easy answer to our question is a *legal* duty, a duty internal to the system of norms that is law. These legal duties are just one of many kinds of duties internal to many kinds of normative systems, from small clubs and associations to societal codes of conduct. All such duties can be referred to as "institutional," "positional," or "conventional" duties. The existence of these kinds of duties is a simple function of what is required by the rules or conventions according to which the institutions or organizations operate.

The question to be addressed here, however, has to do not with the existence of such institutional duties (which nobody questions), but rather with their moral weight. Our question is whether or not there is a *moral* duty to discharge our assigned legal duties, and if so, why. We want to know whether there is an external, neutral moral duty (or obligation) to discharge the internal

I am grateful to Ray Frey, Nancy Schauber, and David Tabachnick for their helpful comments on earlier versions of this essay.

duties imposed by law.[1] In the case of a moral duty, its normative force derives from independent moral principles beyond any
conventional or institutional "force" that might be thought generated by the simple empirical facts of institutional requirement
(according to existing rules) or widespread social expectations for
conduct. Our question, then, is why (or whether) one has a moral
duty to do what the rules require or what society expects. And on
that question, of course, there is room for debate, just as there is
room for debate about whether or not it is morally required that
we follow the rules of other particular groups that might try to
claim our obedience as their due. Institutional and organizational
claims are plainly not self-justifying. What, then, is the moral justification for the claim to obedience made by the institutions of a
formal domestic legal system?

In the case of many laws, of course, it may seem that the moral
requirement to obey the law is every bit as plain as the existence
of the external, neutral moral duties that are to explain the duty to
obey. For much of the law seems to be devoted simply to enforcing
morality. The criminal law prohibitions of (for example) murder,
assault, fraud, and theft can be seen as just institutionalizing (and
enforcing with the threat of formal sanctions) the parallel moral
prohibitions. Much of the body of contract law mirrors the morality of promising, just as some of tort law follows common views
of the morality of reparation. But while it is perhaps plain in these
cases that there is a moral duty or obligation to do (or to remit)
what the law requires, this duty should not be seen as equivalent to a duty to *obey* the law. I do not *obey* a military superior
when I decide on completely independent grounds to do what

---

1 In this essay I will not be concerned with any differences between moral *duties*
and moral *obligations*. I will assume that accounting for a general obligation
to obey the law would be fully as satisfying to all of the relevant theorists as
would accounting for a general duty to obey. On the differences between duties
and obligations, see my *Moral Principles and Political Obligations* (Princeton, NJ:
Princeton University Press, 1979), 11–16. On the idea of "external" duties or
justifications, see my "External Justifications and Institutional Roles," in *Justification and Legitimacy: Essays on Rights and Obligations* (Cambridge: Cambridge
University Press, 2001).

he happens to have commanded (as when I retreat from mere prudence or cowardice at the same time that he happens to be ordering a retreat). Obedience essentially concerns the source of a rule or command, not its content. I obey my military superior's command to do C when I do C because he commands that I do C, not because I am independently inclined to do C. (These are the "surrender of judgment" and the "content independence" that subjection to authoritative commands is often said to involve.) A moral duty to obey the law would be a duty to do as the law requires *because* it is required by valid law (or because of what its being valid law implies), a duty to obey the law as such, not to do as it requires just insofar as it happens to overlap with independent moral duties (which should be discharged whether or not they are also made legal duties). Now I certainly do not intend to suggest, of course, that it is simply a coincidence that the law in many respects reflects the considered moral views of those from whom it demands obedience. But I do mean to emphasize that our question in this essay concerns the general moral authority of our laws, not just the extent to which law rides piggyback on prior and freestanding duties of morality.

Understanding in this way our question, "Is there a duty to obey the law?", we can see immediately that the answer is unlikely to be a simple "Yes." Any affirmative answer will certainly be heavily qualified. For not only do different legal systems differ in the specific legal duties they impose, different laws even within particular legal systems typically seem differentially morally binding. Few theorists would be inclined to defend a moral duty to obey laws requiring the capture and return of fugitive slaves or requiring that we provide information to the authorities that will send morally innocent persons to death camps, even if in other respects the legal systems that imposed such requirements were exemplary. More generally (and less dramatically), even legal systems that are quite just on balance typically include at least some laws with respect to which even the most convinced proponent of a general moral duty to obey the law will have some doubts. Some theorists are motivated by such cases to qualify their answers by asserting the existence of a prima facie duty to obey the law, a duty that can be overridden in the case of intolerably unjust laws, or a tentative duty that is only *actually* a duty where such moral objections to law are not present.

But even if we accept this strategy, it still seems clear that any answer to our general question about a duty to obey the law will have to be loaded with caveats and qualifications. For not only are vile and deeply unjust systems of law not owed even a prima facie moral duty of obedience, even within generally just societies various persons are likely to stand in rather different moral relations to the law. Those who have without good cause suffered disproportionately the burdens imposed by unjust law, or those who have without cause been denied enjoyment of the benefits law provides (think, for instance, of minority groups in moderately biased societies or persons living in isolated or inadequately policed territories), may well have very different duties with respect to the law than do citizens in more normal or happier circumstances. Indeed, individuals could differ in their duties simply because of quite personal and idiosyncratic moral relationships into which they might have entered. (I might, say, have a moral duty to obey the law because I made a sincere promise to my mother that I would do so.) We are interested in answers to our question that are of sufficient generality to apply to many members of real societies while at the same time being sufficiently qualified and fine-grained so as to account for obvious facts about the morally relevant differences between both different kinds of legal systems and persons in different circumstances within particular societies. In attempting to answer our question, we will thus undoubtedly find ourselves often thinking about the answer only for certain kinds of (decent) legal systems and for most persons within communities governed by such systems.

"Is there a duty to obey the law?" is, of course, not only among the oldest and most enduring of philosophical questions, but a question that has continued to attract the attention of legal, social, and political philosophers. A wide variety of accounts of the nature and source of our duty to obey is currently on offer, with all such accounts opposed not only by proponents of alternative accounts, but also by an array of skeptics who deny the existence (and, in some cases, even the possibility) of such duties. Academic lawyers and political scientists are as fully engaged in the debates as are philosophers. One explanation for this attention is that answers to questions about the duty to obey the law seem to have quite immediate practical implications for our everyday lives. These questions are one of the points at which political (and legal) philosophy makes its most obvious contact with the concerns of thoughtful laypersons. We may, for instance, care deeply about liberty or justice (about the division of property in our society, about its form of government and institutional means for resolving political differences, about the proper limits on individual liberty and the correct role for cultural identities, and so on); and we may care deeply as a result about the character of the laws and the political institutions under which we live. But we are seldom in a position, individually or in small groups, to have much effect on whether our laws and institutions live up to our cherished ideals. By contrast, we all face, individually and regularly, questions about whether to obey the law (and, by extension, whether to vote in elections, support our governments, demonstrate patriotic allegiance, and the like). These are all questions that are addressed, even if not necessarily fully resolved, by solutions to the problem of the duty to obey the law. Is it really wrong to break this law, even if I can easily escape punishment for the breach and even if nobody else will be obviously harmed by my disobedience? Is there really a moral duty not to exceed the speed limit or drive while intoxicated, not to cheat on our taxes or use illegal recreational substances, not to evade jury duty or registration for the military draft? Many persons, both within and without the academy, are plainly (and plainly ought to be) interested in such practical questions, if for no other reason than that most of us take our perceived moral duties and obligations at least reasonably seriously.[2]

---

2 Here I disagree with Allen Buchanan's claims that an account of "political authority," along with the correlative notion of an obligation to obey, is not important to the central issues of political philosophy (*Justice, Legitimacy, and Self-Determination* [Oxford: Oxford University Press, 2004], 237–41). At times

Much obedience to law (and support for domestic governments), of course, is motivated by fear of legal sanctions, by childhood training and habit, and by a variety of nonrational attachments to community, nation, or state. Both philosophers and laypersons, however, frequently aver that in addition to these prudential reasons and nonrational motivations to obey the law, there are rational moral grounds for demanding from them legal obedience. Indeed, I think it is likely true that most of us living in reasonably just societies believe that there is a general moral duty to comply with the requirements of valid domestic law (or at least would *say*, with appropriate prompting, that we believe in such a duty[3]). But even if most ordinary people do in fact feel duty-bound in this way, we should not be too hasty in taking such feelings as plainly justified (i.e., as accurately tracking our true moral duties) unless we can support those feelings by reference to some recognizable line of moral reasoning.

After all, people do sometimes feel morally required to act in ways that we surely cannot want to say reflect their actual moral duties – for example, the downtrodden poor man who feels

---

Buchanan seems to mean by this only that an account of a duty owed *to government* is unimportant, since he appears to regard as important the possibility of a duty owed to fellow citizens (ibid., 253–6). But if (as Locke thought and as I believe) a *people* can hold political authority, then a duty owed to fellow citizens *is* a duty that correlates with (their) political authority. At other times (e.g., 239–40), however, Buchanan (citing me) plainly wants to argue that since other kinds of moral, prudential, or personal reasons for legal compliance will exist regardless, demonstrating as well a duty to obey is simply unnecessary to reasonable concerns in political philosophy. This also seems to me false. While we may certainly often (though, just as certainly, not always) have reasons to comply independent of a duty to obey, it is the duty to obey that must be invoked to explain why it is morally wrong for us to compete with our authorities or to decline political association with those around us. (An account of why governments are simply justified in acting as they do – of the sort offered by Buchanan – will not suffice to explain this.) As we will see, it is on precisely these points that Natural Duty theories like Buchanan's founder.

3 Leslie Green raises reasonable doubts about whether such assertions of belief might in fact indicate rather different commitments than would at first seem to be the case. See "Who Believes in Political Obligation?" in W. A. Edmundson (ed.), *The Duty to Obey the Law* (Lanham, MD: Rowman & Littlefield, 1999).

duty-bound to defer to his social "betters" (or the black man who feels he must defer to whites) or the brainwashed political prisoner who is brought to feel duty-bound in exactly the ways his tormenters intended (or conditioned creatures of duty, analogous to those of Huxley's *Brave New World*). Especially where relations of domination and subjection are at issue, as they certainly are in all organized political societies with functioning legal systems, we should be extremely wary of trying to defend judgments about moral duty by simple appeal to the feelings of the subjects – feelings of duty that may be straightforward components of "false consciousness" or perhaps just uncritically accepted sentiments of loyalty to the dominant authorities in one's domain. While appeal to widely shared, thoughtfully considered, critically examined judgments of moral duty by ordinary persons may well be a defensible starting point in moral theorizing, it is plainly not defensible to begin by appealing to judgments that seem likely to be distorted in their genesis or development – for instance, by appealing to feelings that arose in circumstances that render those specific feelings inherently suspicious. I would contend that any "sense of duty" to law or polity that arises within the hierarchical, coercive framework of legal and political relations that characterizes the modern state cannot be regarded as safe from such reasonable suspicions. The clear instrumental value to political and legal superiors (and, more generally, to those enjoying positions of privilege) of an inculcated popular sense of duty to obey, along with the wide variety of means of inculcation available to leaders and to the privileged in modern states, are the obvious sources of such suspicions.

If, indeed, most people do regard themselves as subject to a moral duty to obey the law, then we would do well to let that be the first word in our inquiry, not the last, and to explore carefully the lines of argument that might lead us to view such judgments as well justified.[4] Traditionally, of course, discussions of the moral

---

4 It is not, of course, uncommon, especially in social-scientific discussions of legitimacy, to try to characterize state legitimacy – and, presumably, citizens' correlative duties to obey – precisely in terms of dominant attitudes toward

duty to obey the law have been deeply conservative in character. Their objective has been less to explore the question of *whether* such a duty exists than to try to explain or justify the dominant belief in the existence of such a duty, and they would have been viewed simply as failures had they concluded without proposing such an explanation or justification. My approach in this essay, as I have already suggested, will not be conservative in this way. Nor will it be guided by the traditional insistence on finding a "one size fits all" answer, either positive or negative. It might well turn out to be true (again, as suggested earlier) that even within a single reasonably just society, many persons have a moral duty to obey the law, while many others do not. Or it might be that typical citizens in familiar states have a moral duty to obey, but that this duty binds them more narrowly (or broadly) than they or their governments suppose. Or, of course, it might be that anarchists have been correct in insisting that all (possible or actual) citizens of all (possible or actual) states lack even a narrow moral duty to obey the law. In short, I will not regard my enterprise here as failed simply by virtue of its inability to confirm any of our pretheoretical beliefs on the subject of a duty to obey. These beliefs are not, in my view, sufficiently reliable to stand as data to which any respectable theory must conform. The only standard of success acknowledged in this essay will be that its conclusions should follow from good arguments.

Of course, if our conclusions challenge these pretheoretical beliefs about a duty to obey the law, they will inevitably challenge as well a variety of associated views about the nature of our relationships to our legal and political institutions. But they will, I think,

---

the state among citizens. On such accounts, legitimate authority is ascribed to states or regimes whose subjects feel toward them loyalty, allegiance, or other kinds of approval, or to states or regimes with the capacities to generate such feelings. But it is easy to see that this sort of account implies, implausibly, that states can acquire or enhance *legitimacy* by misleading or by indoctrinating their subjects, or on the strength of subjects' extraordinary stupidity, immorality, or imprudence. Legitimacy and the duty to obey must surely turn not on the attitudes of subjects, but rather on facts about the state's history, character, or relations with its subjects. See my "Justification and Legitimacy," 131–5 (in *Justification and Legitimacy*).

challenge less dramatically than we might expect our normal understanding of when morality dictates conformity with law and political nonresistance. Since my coauthor, Christopher Wellman, takes issue specifically with this claim, however (taking me to have misconceived the relationship between political and philosophical anarchism), I will reserve my response on this subject for Chapter 8 (after we have examined Wellman's own views).

As my remarks thus far have suggested, in this essay I will argue against the existence of a widespread duty to obey the law, even in reasonably just political societies (like those in which most of my readers undoubtedly reside). My ultimate goal is to extend and solidify my previous defenses of the (philosophical anarchist's) view that the mere fact that an action is legally required or that a stable government holds power within a reasonably just state is insufficient to establish a moral presumption in favor of legal compliance. Because, however, I believe that no a priori arguments are available to demonstrate the *impossibility* of a duty to obey (indeed, I believe that small numbers of actual persons have such a duty), my case against a general duty to obey must proceed by showing how the various possible theories of the duty to obey either fail in their own terms or fail to apply to – that is, fail to explain or justify the alleged duties of – most real citizens of real states.

In a volume of this length, I cannot possibly deal in detail with all of the plausible or popular theories of the duty to obey the law. My strategy, accordingly, will be to focus on one prominent tradition of thought on the subject while offering relatively brief summaries of the arguments that seem to me to discredit rival accounts. The tradition on which I will concentrate is, I believe, the most influential among contemporary political and legal theorists: namely, (what I will call) the Natural Duty family of theories, which prominently includes Kant's theory, along with its contemporary neo-Kantian/Rawlsian offspring. That family (or tradition of thought) will be the subject of Chapter 7 of this essay. In Chapter 6, I will first briefly examine the other families of rival theories.

6   The Theories

Three Families

In the discussion that follows, I will defend a division of the available theories of the duty to obey the law into three groups or "families."[1] This division will allow me (in this section) to discuss the merits and difficulties of two of these families briefly and in very general terms, largely summarizing arguments that I have made before. In particular, I will distinguish (what I call) Associative, Transactional, and Natural Duty theories of a duty to obey.[2] Associative accounts ground our duty to obey in our nonvoluntary occupation of certain duty-laden social roles, while Transactional accounts ground our duty (or obligation) to obey in our morally significant interactions with our states or fellow citizens. I will attempt (in this chapter) to explain and deal with these first two families of theories by revealing what I take to be the

---

1 The discussion that follows in this section draws heavily on my observations in "Political Obligation and Authority," in Robert L. Simon (ed.), *The Blackwell Guide to Social and Political Philosophy* (Malden, MA: Blackwell, 2002).

2 I do not discuss here what might be considered a fourth family of theories – namely, pluralist theories that utilize aspects of more than one of my three families in their accounts of the duty to obey. In my view, the failures of the three families to account independently for the duty to obey infect any efforts to combine the insights of the various families. If our political societies are not cooperative schemes, then it is not "approximately true" that we owe them obedience as a matter of fairness. It is simply false. Only if each family could account for the duties of a distinct significant minority of citizens could they hope to account collectively for a general duty to obey. My criticisms of the three families of theories are not, however, consistent with such a supposition.

fatal defects that infect all possible members of the families, saving my more detailed discussion and criticism for the last family. Chapter 7 will then be devoted to a much more careful examination of the third – and currently the most popular – of these families of theories. Natural Duty theories of the duty to obey the law are those that ground our duty to obey not in who we are (as in Associative accounts) or in what we've done or enjoyed (as in Transactional accounts), but rather either (a) in the moral importance of advancing some impartial moral good or (b) in some moral duty thought to be owed by all persons to all others as moral equals, regardless of roles, relationships, or transactions. The theories of Kant and contemporary Kantians, consequentialists (e.g., utilitarians or perfectionists), and so-called necessity theorists all fall within this extended family.

The division of families of theories that I propose here is not, I think, especially new or controversial (despite the odd bedfellows it makes of Kantian and utilitarian theories). Indeed, I think the three families can all be found separately represented in even the earliest recorded (and still undoubtedly the best known) treatment of the philosophical problem of the duty to obey. I refer, of course, to Plato's dialogue *Crito*, a discussion of the duty of legal obedience that is now nearly 2,400 years old. *Crito* is Plato's (probably nonfictional) recounting of Socrates' justification for refusing to flee Athens after his trial and death sentence. In defending his decision to stay and die to his friend and follower Crito (who hopes to assist Socrates in escaping into exile), Socrates advances a layered argument, each portion of which is intended to support the conclusion that justice (or right) requires him to remain and obey the unjust command of the Athenian court. This argument is largely presented in Socrates' imagined conversation with the Laws of Athens, and its conclusion is an especially strong one: that Socrates is morally bound to virtually absolute obedience to the law, even where the law wrongly imposes a sentence of death.

In Socrates' conversation with the Laws, at least three kinds of arguments are clearly used and distinguished (and finally summarized) by the Laws to counter the case for disobedience that

Socrates imagines himself and Crito offering to them. The first argument is that the Laws (by which we may understand the state and the society as well) are like a father and master to Socrates, having "begotten, nurtured, and educated" him. These roles of child and servant of the state require Socrates to "either persuade it or do what it commands."[3] The second claim is that the state and the laws, in raising him, have given Socrates a "share of all the fine things" available to it (51d). And the third distinct argument offered by the Laws is that by living in the state without objection, by bringing up children in its territories (and so on), even after "seeing the way in which [the Laws] decide [their] cases in court and the other ways in which [they] manage [their] city," Socrates has, "by his act of staying, agreed with [the Laws] to do what [they] demand of him" (51d–52d).

Notice that the first of the Laws' arguments emphasizes centrally who Socrates *is*. What he owes to the Laws he owes because of his identity, because of roles or positions he occupies. In the same way that we normally suppose a child owes its parents honor and obedience, simply by virtue of occupying the nonvoluntary role ("child" or "offspring"), so Socrates, "begotten," raised, and made who he is by the Laws and the state, finds himself in the unchosen role of the Laws' child and servant, a role that carries with it a duty of honor and obedience. Accounts of the duty to obey the law that appeal in this way to position, role, or identity are the ones that I have called Associative theories.

The Laws' second argument for a duty of obedience points to a different feature of Socrates' situation. This argument emphasizes not who Socrates has become or the roles he plays in the state. It emphasizes instead what Socrates has received from the Laws' workings. Athens has, under the Laws' direction, given Socrates (and all of its other citizens) many significant benefits, some of which Socrates actually mentions but many more of which we can easily imagine. And we normally suppose that the recipients

---

3 *Crito*, 50d–51e. This and subsequent quotations are from the translation of *Crito* in A. D. Woozley, *Law and Obedience* (London: Duckworth, 1979). Subsequent quotations will be identified in the text by standard paginations.

of important benefits owe their benefactors something appropriate in return for that benefaction. In the case of the Laws, the "appropriate something" is, the Laws argue, obedience and support.

Finally, in the third argument noted earlier, the Laws point not to the ways in which Socrates has benefited from the Laws, but instead to what Socrates has freely *done*. He has freely, if only tacitly or implicitly, consented or agreed to abide by the verdicts of Athens' courts. His consent presumably is supposed to have been given as well to the other basic ways in which the city is managed. We all agree, of course, that persons have a moral obligation to honor their promises and voluntary undertakings. And Socrates' promise to obey was even clearer than that of many other Athenians, the Laws contend, since he demonstrated his satisfaction with Athens not only by remaining there when he might have freely emigrated, but also by virtually never leaving the city, by raising a family there, and so on.

The second and third arguments employed by Socrates (through the mouth of the Laws) both appeal to the nature of Socrates' morally significant interactions or "transactions"[4] with the Laws or the city-state. Athens has benefited Socrates in significant ways. Socrates has promised or agreed to obey the Laws and support the state. While the second of these transactions (the promise) is necessarily voluntary (if it is to be binding), and the first (the benefaction) need not be, both arguments revolve around political transactions, morally significant things that have been done by or for Socrates. Accounts of the duty to obey that ground the duty in such political transactions are the ones that I have called Transactional accounts.

So the three arguments that are specifically individuated in the Laws' summary of their case all utilize either Associative or Transactional duties or obligations to Athens. And the three arguments

---

4 I use the term "transaction" throughout this essay in a way that ignores one familiar aspect of its meaning – namely, that involving multilateral participation and negotiation. As I use the term here, for instance, benefiting another counts as a transaction even if only one party (the benefactor, say) is aware that the benefaction has occurred.

seem sufficiently general that they are plainly intended to apply not just to Socrates, but to many or all of his fellow citizens as well. Given their generality, it might easily be supposed as well that they apply equally to persons in contemporary political societies. But the Laws' overall argument that Socrates has a duty to obey does not in fact appear to be exhausted by the three kinds of arguments that are actually summarized in *Crito*. Indeed, the very first response made by the Laws to Socrates' proposal that he ignore his legal duty and escape seems to appeal to very different considerations than those we have thus far noted. What the Laws begin by saying is this: "Do you intend to do anything else by this exploit . . . than to destroy both ourselves the laws and the entire city – at least as far as you can?" (50a–b). Since private citizens of Athens cannot all disobey the lawful verdicts of Athenian courts without ultimately endangering the city's survival, Socrates' proposed escape, however innocent it might seem considered by itself, must be taken to be aiming at the impermissible end of Athens' destruction.

Both the location of this argument (at the very start of a discussion that only later mentions the three grounds of his duties) and its wording strongly suggest that it is intended to have force independent of the three other arguments discussed previously. For instance, if it is not *always* wrong to (try to) destroy a state or laws (as we might reasonably suppose, keeping in mind tyrannical or deeply unjust states), perhaps the Laws' idea is that it is wrong to destroy good or just states, of which Athens happens to be one. The goodness or justice of states/laws provides all persons with moral reasons not to aim at their destruction. We know that Socrates takes the Laws of Athens to be blameless in his unjust death sentence, for he accepts their reminder that "as things stand, you will leave here, if you do, wronged not by us the laws but by men" (54c). On this interpretation of the opening argument, then, it is Socrates' duty to be just and to uphold just institutions that bind him not to destroy the Laws (or to aim at that end). The justice or goodness of laws and states grounds a moral duty for all persons to respect or support laws or states with those properties.

On its face, of course, the opening argument appears to have a more consequentialist character than is true of the reading just proposed. Perhaps the idea is simply that Socrates' escape would be wrong because it would have worse consequences than would his remaining to face his legally mandated death sentence. By remaining, Socrates would die, of course (though he seems to regard that as no great evil, either for himself or for his friends); but far worse would be his escape's contribution to the destruction of the Laws and the city. Alternatively, an even more natural consequentialist reading of the text would ascribe to it not a direct consequentialist argument of this sort, but rather a "generalization" argument. Socrates' escape would be wrong because if all others in similar positions acted as he proposes to, then the consequences would be far worse than if all accepted the verdicts of the courts. Only the hypothetical bad consequences of generalized escape, not the actual expected bad consequences in Socrates' particular case, would be necessary (on this reading) to argue for the wrongness of escape.

We will briefly discuss in Chapter 7 the persuasiveness of these kinds of consequentialist arguments. The point for now, however, is that both consequentialist arguments for the duty to obey, as well as the argument from a duty of justice, all seem to utilize at their cores neither Transactional nor Associative "facts" about Socrates and the Laws of Athens. Socrates' duty not to try to destroy the Laws is explained instead by appeal to the moral quality of the Laws or the impartial moral values that his legal obedience will bring about or advance – values such as happiness or justice. Our general duties to advance or respect such values, by (in this case) upholding the institutions that embody and promote them, are what explain the wrongness of Socrates' proposed escape on all three readings of the opening "destruction argument." The theories that in this way ground our duty to obey the law in one (or more) of the general moral duties that we have simply as persons and moral equals are the theories that I referred to previously as Natural Duty theories. This essay is principally devoted to an examination of this last kind of theory of the duty to obey.

Let me try to focus these initial remarks about my proposed division of theories of the duty to obey – and try to make clearer the character of each of the families I've identified – with some relatively elementary observations about the nature of moral requirements. All moral requirements are either general or special. Similarly, all moral requirements are either voluntary or non-voluntary. Moral requirements are general when they bind us simply in virtue of our personhood and moral equality, irrespective of any special roles or relationships into which we may have entered (or in which we may find ourselves) and any particular binding acts we may have performed. The familiar moral duties not to murder, assault, or lie count as general requirements, as do any duties to promote impartial values like justice or happiness. These duties are often said to be owed by us to persons generally – or, in some cases, not to be owed to anyone at all. Special moral requirements, by contrast, are grounded in (or arise within) those special relationships that we have (or freely make) with particular others or groups, and they are owed specifically to those others or groups. So promissory or contractual obligations, obligations to cooperate within social groups, and obligations to friends, family, or neighbors would all count as special moral requirements. Just as familiar is the (related, but not identical) division of moral requirements into those that are voluntary – that is, those that rest on a voluntary performance of our own, such as consent, promise, perhaps free acceptance of benefits, deliberately injuring another, or choosing to create a child – and those that fall on us nonvoluntarily, simply because we are persons or because we occupy some nonvoluntary role or status.

If these two dichotomies are exhaustive (as I believe them to be), then there might at first seem to be four possible classes of moral requirements: general, voluntary; general, nonvoluntary; special, voluntary; and special nonvoluntary. But the first of these possible classes – the general, voluntary moral requirements – seems to me to be internally inconsistent, hence empty. Our voluntary performances cannot ground moral requirements but do so irrespective of our special relationships or performances. The moral significance of our voluntary performances is precisely that they create or constitute special relationships or performances. So let us say instead that all moral requirements fall into one of three classes: general, nonvoluntary; special, voluntary; or special, nonvoluntary.

Now the three families of theories that we have been discussing – Associative, Transactional, and Natural Duty theories – typically employ respectively in their accounts of the duty to obey the three different classes of moral requirements. Associative theories emphasize the nonvoluntary roles or positions we occupy, and so the duty to obey that is supposed to be grounded in these role relationships must be seen as a special, nonvoluntary moral requirement. Transactional theories tend to focus our attention on special, voluntary requirements that bind us to obey, such as those grounded in our promises, our consent, or our free acceptance of cooperatively produced benefits. Transactional theories may also utilize special, nonvoluntary requirements, but only when these requirements arise from real transactions – such as Socrates' receipt of important benefits from the Laws, benefits that he had no real option of refusing (at least until he was old enough to make a decision to emigrate). Lastly, Natural Duty theories employ in their accounts requirements to promote impartial values or requirements that bind us simply because we are persons. They must, then, identify our duty to obey the law with some kind of general, nonvoluntary moral requirement.

These observations about the three families of theories, elementary though they may be, allow us to see clearly a couple of important points about the theoretical obstacles that the theories in question will have to overcome. First, Associative and Natural Duty theories seem to have an advantage over (at least) voluntaristic Transactional theories in one way that their answers (to our question about the duty to obey the law) square with ordinary conceptions of the duty to obey. For few nontheorists, I would guess, think that their duty to obey the law is contingent on their having performed some voluntary undertaking to bring themselves under the law's authority. Our duty to obey seems to most persons to be a relatively basic, nonvoluntary feature of our moral lives (analogous, perhaps, to familial duties), just as Associative and Natural Duty theories aver.

Second, however, it is Associative and Transactional theories that appear to have a clear initial advantage over Natural Duty theories in a different way that their answers fit ordinary conceptions of the duty to obey. Both Associative and Transactional theories claim that our duty to obey is a *special* moral requirement. Our duty will thus be owed to some particular association, group, or person, depending upon the associative roles we occupy or the transactions in which we have been involved. Natural Duty theories, by contrast, have to understand our duty to obey as a general requirement, one that binds us irrespective of the special features of our lives, and one that is owed to persons generally. But our duty to obey the law is most often understood as a duty to obey *domestic* law, as a moral requirement that binds us specially to our own laws (countries, governments, states, etc.), based in the special relationship we have to one particular legal system. It seems clear that Associative and Transactional theories, by appealing to special moral requirements to explain the duty to obey, can easily explain this feature of ordinary thought about that duty in a way that Natural Duty theories cannot. How can we have a natural duty, one based in our personhood and owed to all others, that nonetheless ties us specially to one particular institution in one particular social group? This special problem for Natural Duty theories of the duty to obey is what I have called the problem of "particularity," and I will return to it at considerable length in Chapter 7 of this essay.

It may seem from these initial points that Associative theories or nonvoluntaristic Transactional theories of the duty to obey are the obvious places to look for our answer, since those kinds of theories square with commonsense views of the duty in both of the ways just noted. The duties they identify as relevant to required legal obedience are (or can be) both nonvoluntary and special. But, as we will see, these initially promising theories face serious problems of other sorts. I begin with the Associative family of theories, reminding the reader that I intend to give here only the barest outline of the difficulties that I (and others) have already identified. I will then proceed to give the Transactional family of theories the same kind of quick treatment, trusting that readers dissatisfied with this brevity will be willing to explore further the more careful and thorough work cited in the footnotes.

Associative Theories

Associative theories of the duty to obey the law, as we have seen, try to rest the relevant moral duty on basic facts about persons' identities or facts about the legal, social, or political roles they occupy. These theories are familiar to us today chiefly in the work of communitarian theorists, themselves routinely inspired by the work of Aristotle, Burke, Hegel, or Wittgenstein. But at least one influential liberal theorist – Ronald Dworkin – has also defended an Associative theory of our duty to obey domestic law.[5] We have seen part of what makes Associative theories initially attractive: namely, the way in which they purport to explain the duty to obey as a nonvoluntary but still special duty (or obligation). But the principal, and in my view fatal, defect of such theories is also displayed plainly on their faces: The claims about our moral duties or obligations made by Associative theories are (and need to be) either too strong to be plausible or too similar to the claims made in Transactional or Natural Duty theories to be interestingly distinguishable from them. Thus, Associative theories are hung on the horns of a dilemma. They must either make claims that are counterintuitive and indefensible, or (once their claims are rendered plausible) they must collapse into some kind of non-Associative theory.[6]

5 Ronald Dworkin, *Law's Empire* (Cambridge, MA: Harvard University Press, 1986), 195–215.
6 The arguments of this section largely reproduce (in vastly more compact form) those I made in "Associative Political Obligations" and "External Justifications and Institutional Roles," both in my *Justification and Legitimacy*. For another (also skeptical) take on the relevance of Associative obligations to central questions in political philosophy, see the following papers by Christopher Wellman: "Associative Allegiances and Political Obligations" (*Social Theory and Practice* 23 [1997]), "Relational Facts in Liberal Political Theory: Is There Magic in the

In some versions of the Associative approach, the claims made are wildly strong: It is alleged to be analytic or to be a conceptual truth that citizens are subject to the authority of their states and have a duty to obey domestic law. But, depending on how such claims are intended, these uses of the Associative strategy can be easily shown to be either implausible or simply irrelevant. Nobody believes (or should believe) that just anyone who has been assigned by domestic rule or practice the legal position of "citizen" in any kind of state is morally bound to obedience. States can be monstrously unjust and oppressive or clearly illegitimate, and they can name whomever they please as their citizens (including persons living beyond their internationally accepted jurisdictions). But if we modify the argument to claim that only those are bound to obey who are legitimately subject to the authority of their legal and political institutions, then we have claimed something true (indeed, something analytic) at the cost of claiming something utterly uninteresting; for we have said nothing at all about what it is that *makes* a person legitimately subject to some state's authority, which is the real issue that our three families of theories need to address.

More convincing Associative theories have made weaker and more interesting claims about our moral duties. But in all such cases, even moderately careful specification of the moral claims employed in the theories shows them to be in fact indistinguishable from those employed in Transactional and Natural Duty theories. Associative theories cannot, therefore, enjoy any of the advantages over those other two families of theories that their proponents allege (or imply). In previous discussions of these weaker Associative theories, I have divided them into three groups: what I've called "nonvoluntarist contract theories," "identity theories," and "normative independence theories."

Pronoun 'My'?" (*Ethics* 110 [2000]), "Friends, Compatriots, and Special Political Obligations" (*Political Theory* 29 [2001]). See also Leslie Green, "Associative Obligations and the State," in Allan C. Hutchinson and Leslie Green (eds.), *Law and the Community* (Toronto: Carswell, 1989) and Philip Soper, *The Ethics of Deference* (Cambridge: Cambridge University Press, 2002), 169–72.

According to the first of these – the nonvoluntarist contract theories – citizens of normal political societies simply grow into networks of expectation and commitment that jointly define a kind of nonvoluntary, but nonetheless binding, contract with one another to act as good citizens of that society (by, for example, obeying the law and in other ways upholding the authority of the state). But these theories must fail doubly to achieve their goals. First, insofar as they appeal to the moral requirements arising from our commitments, they are plainly Transactional in inspiration, not Associative. And insofar as they appeal to moral requirements arising from others' expectations, these theories must be either utilitarian (hence Natural Duty theories) or simply non-explanatory: for others' expectations clearly do not impose on us moral duties unless those expectations are legitimate (it is psychologically possible for me to expect of you anything my heart desires); and that leaves the interesting work of explaining what *makes* others' expectations legitimate undone (with the most plausible solutions again being to appeal to Transactional or Natural Duty bases for expectation). Second, while nonvoluntarist contract theories may seem (but, in my view, ultimately are not) well equipped to address questions about the obligations that friends and neighbors might owe one another, they are utterly incapable of explaining how members of a large-scale, pluralistic political community could be taken to owe obligations to all of their fellow citizens (or to their state generally); for the interactions of typical members, hence their opportunities for commitment and for raising expectations, are routinely quite local, not national. And, in any event, expectation theories seem ill equipped to explain general moral duties to obey the law.[7]

Identity theories (the second class of Associative theories) attempt to explain our moral duty to obey domestic law by noting the practical incoherence of denying certain aspects of our identities, such as our roles as duty-bound members of a particular

---

7 See William O. Edmundson, *Three Anarchical Fallacies* (Cambridge: Cambridge University Press, 1998), 21–4. Edmundson equates Associative theories with expectation accounts, which seems to me a mistake. But his critique of expectation accounts seems sound.

political community. Such roles are taken by many persons, the argument goes, to be absolutely central to their sense of who they are; persons cannot coherently simply reject the roles that define them or the duties bound up in those roles. But again, the argument proves either too little or too much. It is not at all clear why we should believe that mere identification with a duty-laden social role is sufficient to ground genuine moral duties. The mere fact that, for example, one's role as citizen of the Third Reich is central to one's practical identity surely does not show that one has a moral duty to discharge all of the institutional duties associated with that role (such as the legal duty to reveal the hiding places of Jews). Only, it seems, when our social and political roles are themselves morally defensible (and non-refusable by those unwilling to occupy them) could the duties associated with them be taken to be morally binding. But that simply returns us once again to the prior issue of the right kinds of arguments to use for demonstrating the moral authority of certain kinds of legal and political arrangements. Identification with a social role is either morally uninteresting or becomes interesting only after the questions with which we are here concerned (about the moral duties associated with social roles) have already been answered.

The last of the three kinds of Associative approaches – normative independence theories – simply affirms what the preceding arguments implicitly reject: namely, the normative authority of local practices. If the source of (some) genuine moral requirements is just their assignment to individuals by local social, legal, and political practices, then there is good reason to suppose that a general duty to obey the law might be among these genuine requirements, given the widespread local social expectations of compliance with and support for the legal and political institutions of our states of residence. But to accept this style of argument is to accept that the mere social instantiation of a practice, independent of any externally justifying point or virtues of that practice, is sufficient to make that practice's rules generate genuine moral requirements for those held subject to the rules. And to accept that, I think, is to reduce the relevant idea of a moral *justification* for claims of duty to nothing at all. Something cannot count as a justification of P if it does not claim for P some special point, advantage, or virtue. But once the Associative theorist allows that only externally justified practices can define genuine moral requirements, then he owes us an explanation of why we should regard the practice, rather than the values that certify it, as the source of the relevant moral requirements. As far as I can see, such explanations are unforthcoming from Associative theories, likely for the simple reason that requirements that are defined *internally* in social practices (like those of politics and law) cannot be morally justified in any plausible or recognizable way without appeal to *external* moral considerations. And any appeal to such external considerations will transform the theory from an Associative theory to one actually based in Transactional or Natural Duty claims. Associative theories of the duty to obey must, to make their claims of moral duty plausible, transform themselves into non-Associative ones.

Transactional Theories

The great weakness of the Associative theories, then, lies in the unpersuasive (or entirely absent) defenses of the moral principles on which they rely in their accounts of the duty to obey. There is simply no good reason to believe that the alleged moral duties or obligations that they utilize in their accounts are in fact real moral duties or obligations at all. This area of greatest weakness in the Associative theories is, by contrast, the greatest area of strength for Transactional theories. By and large, Transactional theories appeal in their accounts of the duty to obey to kinds of moral obligations or duties that are virtually universally accepted as genuine. This is most apparent in the most familiar kind of Transactional theory, which utilizes the obligations arising from consent, contract, or promise to explain the moral duty to obey the law. Few moral obligations or duties are acknowledged by more people than are the moral requirements arising from voluntary undertakings and agreements; for instance, even criminal gangs, warring armies or nations, and so on, which may dismiss

virtually all other moral duties, often still seem to regard themselves as bound by their agreements.

Transactional theories of the duty to obey have generally been
either consent theories or reciprocation theories. According to
consent theories, our duty to obey arises from those of our deliberate acts that constitute voluntary undertakings or agreements.
The consent theory was given its first clear formulation by Locke
and is appealed to in the foundational political documents of
many modern nations (including the American Declaration of
Independence). Reciprocation theories, by contrast, locate the
source of our duty to obey in our responsibilities to reciprocate
for the benefits we accept or receive from our legal systems, governments, or fellow citizens. Reciprocation theories, like consent
theories, are transactional in character. Both concern morally significant interactions with legal and political institutions (or fellow
citizens). Both concern what has been done by or for the citizen.
And both capture much commonsense thinking about our duty
to obey domestic law, as we saw in Socrates' imagined debate
with the Laws. It is easy enough to identify the benefits that flow
to us from living under law, as well as the ways in which our continuing to do so might be taken to involve an implicit agreement
to obey that law. Despite their appeal to common sense, however, both varieties of Transactional theory face by-now-familiar
obstacles.[8]

The different kinds of consent theories can be distinguished
most clearly by attending to the varieties of consent to which
they appeal in their arguments. The simplest and most intuitive
sort of consent theory appeals to the *actual, personal* consent of
individuals in order to explain their moral duties (or obligations)
to obey the law. When you freely agree to obey, you are morally

---

8 The arguments of this section follow those I have previously made in *Moral
Principles and Political Obligations*, Chapters IV, V, and VII; *On the Edge of Anarchy:
Locke, Consent, and the Limits of Society* (Princeton, NJ: Princeton University Press,
1993), Chapter 8; and "Fair Play and Political Obligation: Twenty Years Later,"
in *Justification and Legitimacy*. For the many defenses (and alternative critiques)
of Transactional accounts of the duty to obey (which are too numerous to list
here), see the notes in these works.

bound to do so. Actual consent can be either express (e.g., the consent explicitly given in a promise, a contract, or an oath) or tacit (where acts whose conventional point is not solely that of giving consent acquire the significance of consent by virtue of special contexts in which they are performed[9]). Both kinds of actual consent plainly can ground moral obligations, though some theorists (notably Locke) have thought that express consent binds us more extensively or permanently than does tacit consent. It is not uncommon, however, to appeal as well or instead to certain kinds of *nonactual* consent in attempting to explain the citizen's duty to obey. For instance, *hypothetical* consent (or hypothetical contract) theories purport to derive our obligations to obey from the consent that would be given by some idealized version of ourselves, ranging from versions of ourselves that are merely purged of obvious defects to versions of ourselves that are perfectly rational (and motivationally simplified).

In my view, hypothetical consent theories are in fact best understood as disguised Natural Duty theories rather than as Transactional theories, despite their use of the language of consent. For the entire point of appealing to the consent of idealized persons, instead of that of actual persons, is to emphasize that our obligation to obey does not flow from any transactions with our states into which our flawed and irrational selves might have entered. That obligation derives instead from the virtues or morally important qualities of our states that would elicit the consent of ideal persons (who would rightly perceive and appreciate true virtue or goodness in a way that actual persons often do not). Actual consent theories, then, seem to be the only genuinely transactional form of consent theory.

But however clearly we might perceive the moral obligations that arise from actual consent, actual consent theories of our duty to obey the law confront serious and well-known difficulties:

---

9 Some acts (like saying "I promise" or "I agree" or "I pledge") have as part of their default conventional significance consenting to new obligations. Other acts, like remaining silent, have no clear linguistic/conventional significance. But remaining silent can be a way of (tacitly) giving consent in certain contexts, such as when it constitutes a free, deliberate response to a call for dissent.

most obviously, difficulties in terms of realism. Real citizens in real political communities seldom do anything that can be plausibly described as either a promise to obey or any other kind of freely made commitment to comply with domestic laws. Political life offers very few occasions for making explicit oaths of obedience or allegiance, except in the cases of naturalized citizens or in contexts that are plainly tainted with threats of state coercion. The free political act that perhaps most resembles consent (among those acts performed by many citizens, at least in democracies) is that of voting in democratic elections. But voting is done against a conventional background that strongly implies that such acts *cannot* be taken as the source of any duty to obey the law or support the government. For those duties are clearly represented as both preceding the act of voting – indeed, voting is often seen precisely as part of the content of citizens' duty of support (and is actually legally required in some democracies) – and as in no way diminished or eliminated by citizens' declining to participate in elections (as, of course, significant minorities and occasional majorities in existing democracies routinely do).

Turning to more tacit consensual acts, it proves just as difficult to identify any kind of act that is performed by most real citizens in decent states that could be plausibly understood as an act of tacit consent to obey the law or support the government. Mere continued residence (Locke's famous suggestion) or nonresistance, for instance, while widely practiced, are in fact remarkably bad candidates for acts of consent to obey. For many citizens there are few acceptable options to remaining in their states and obeying (most) law, and for most persons active resistance to the state is in effect impossible. And for none of us is there any option to living in some state or other, all of which make (at least) the same core demands on us. These facts raise serious doubts about the voluntariness of any widely performed acts that might be alleged to be binding acts of political consent. And in the absence of an adequate level of voluntariness, such acts simply cannot be counted as grounding moral duties to obey the law.

If Transactional consent theories fail in these ways to explain a general duty of legal compliance, Transactional reciprocation theories, in my view, fare no better. These latter theories can be divided into two principal groups: those that appeal to our duties or obligations to be *fair* and those that appeal to so-called debts of *gratitude* (or to some simple duty of return for benefits conferred). Broadly speaking, fairness theories hold that persons who benefit from the cooperative sacrifices of others, made in support of a mutually beneficial scheme, have a moral obligation to bear their own fair share of the burdens assigned within that scheme. Taking the benefits of cooperation without doing one's part in the scheme that produces them is to unfairly ride free, to take advantage of others. Gratitude theories hold more simply that we have a moral duty to make appropriate returns for the benefits provided us by others. Political life in decent states plainly involves both a grand, mutually beneficial scheme and the provision of important benefits. Thus, both styles of reciprocation theory seem prima facie promising.

But gratitude theories of a duty to obey collapse rapidly under even the most charitable analysis of moral debts of gratitude. Even if it were true that we owed others a return for the unsolicited benefits they provided, it would not be possible to plausibly char- acterize the contents of such moral debts in any way that would help establish a duty of domestic legal obedience. Suppose that we do in fact owe benefactors a fitting return of some sort. What- ever else may be true of these debts, it is clear, first, that debts of gratitude are only owed to benefactors who have acted with certain motives and, second, that our benefactors are not enti- tled to themselves specify what shall constitute a fitting return. I am owed nothing if I accidentally benefit you while attempt- ing to wrongfully harm you, for example; and I may not provide you with benefits and then simply name my reward. But the motives of states and legal systems when they benefit us are at best mixed or obscure (and it is quite possibly unintelligible to assign motives at all to such mechanical, institutional benefac- tions). Further, obedience to law, as we have seen, is compliance specifically in response to the fact that compliance is required by law. The state is in the business of saying how we shall behave, of saying what our "fitting return" shall be. It cannot, then, hope to characterize its demands as the content of a debt of gratitude. And, given the minimal cost of extending the benefits of law and government to one additional person, a fitting return for such benefits might plausibly be thought to be different from or less than simple obedience to law.

Fairness theories have recently been more popular than gratitude theories among reciprocation theorists, largely due to the influence of Hart and Rawls. But even Rawls came to reject the fairness theory he once supported, arguing that duties of fairness only arise where the benefits of cooperative schemes are freely accepted, and that persons in real political societies seldom freely accept the benefits their societies provide (having no real choice in the matter). Typical citizens can thus not reasonably be thought to be treating others unfairly if they decline to reciprocate. Attempts to avoid Rawls' objection by allowing that even benefits we have not freely accepted obligate us to reciprocate invariably either collapse the fairness theory back into a simple (inadequate) gratitude theory or turn it into a Natural Duty account by stressing not fairness, but rather the impartial moral value of the benefits states and legal systems provide. In any event, we should surely question whether the model on which fairness theories rely in motivating their accounts of our moral obligations – namely, that of small-scale cooperative ventures among face-to-face associates – can in any way be realistically applied to the entities at issue in a theory of our duty to obey the law: namely, very-large-scale, pluralistic, loosely associated polities marked by social, regional, economic, or racial divisions.[10]

---

10 Each of the accounts of our duty to obey the law that I discuss here – Natural Duty, Associative, and Transactional – can, of course, be defended in a less conservative form than is suggested in the text. That is, all such accounts can be defended as the correct account of any duty to obey that persons might actually have, but with the admission that few actual persons have such a duty. My own view, for example, is that actual consent is the only possible ground of a moral duty to obey the law (so that actual consent theory is in this sense the correct account of our duty to obey) but that very few real citizens have given their consent. Especially in light of the problems facing all of the argumentative strategies discussed in this essay, less conservative approaches to the problem of this sort seem especially attractive.

7 Natural Duties and the Duty to Obey the Law

The Basic Argument

The failure of Transactional and Associative theories to explain the source of a general duty to obey domestic law pushes us to explore other possibilities. In particular, since the moral duty to obey seems to many a relatively basic, natural, nonvoluntary feature of social life, it seems initially promising to suppose that the moral principle that accounts for this duty belongs to that group of principles that specifies our natural moral duties. Natural Duty theories of the duty to obey the law, as we have seen, are those that ground our duty to obey not in who we are (as in Associative accounts) or in what we've done or enjoyed (as in Transactional accounts), but rather either (a) in the moral importance of advancing some impartial moral good or (b) in some moral duty thought to be owed by all persons to all others as moral equals, regardless of roles, relationships, or transactions. Thus, the natural duty in question, from which the duty to obey is to be derived, could be a consequentialist moral duty to promote or maximize the occurrence of some good property or state of affairs – such as happiness (utility, preference satisfaction, etc.), moral perfection, or justice. Or the duty could simply be one of that class of moral duties generally thought to be owed by all persons to all other persons just in virtue of their being persons – such as the duties to refrain from violence and deception (e.g., assault, murder, theft, lying) or the duties of justice, charity, mutual aid, or rescue.

I will concentrate most of my attention here on the Natural Duty approaches that are broadly Kantian in character. Within the Natural Duty family, these seem to me to be the most compelling, the most numerous, and the most popular among contemporary philosophers and political and legal theorists. I will also comment very quickly, before beginning my exploration of the Kantian theories, on consequentialist approaches to justifying the duty to obey. These approaches, as we have seen, also count (on my preferred way of dividing theories) as Natural Duty theories, though the difficulties they face are more complicated than those faced by the theories we will consider later, and they can receive here only the briefest consideration.

I begin with what I will call for simplicity "the argument." It is (intentionally) a very general, imprecise sort of argument, insufficiently developed for careful evaluation and never defended by anyone (that I know of) in quite this form. Indeed, as presented, its premises are far too vague for it to be said even that its conclusion follows from their conjunction. What I intend to do with the argument is only to try to capture, at least in very general terms, the most important elements of all of the prominent members of the Natural Duty family of theories of the duty to obey the law. All of the Natural Duty approaches can, I think, find something in the argument that hits near the spirit of their account.

The Argument

Premise 1:   Government (political society, law) is necessary for human beings.
(Explanation: Human beings on earth must inevitably interact with one another, the world being spherical and heavily populated. People have a variety of motives and projects that bring them into conflict with one another. Some are naturally aggressive and seek power over others; some interfere with others in competition for scarce resources; some interfere preemptively to better secure their own well-being. Even those guided by exemplary motives frequently disagree about what morality,

right, and justice require and tend to be biased in favor of themselves and those close to them; and these disagreements further set the stage for conflict. Lack of power and neutrality, along with various coordination and assurance problems, prevent persons from solving these problems themselves in a nonpolitical condition. As a result, without coercive law and government (to settle disagreements about what ought to be done, and to deter and control those who would for these [and other] reasons introduce conflict into human affairs), the human condition would inevitably include the constant threat of war and anarchy; consequent great insecurity of person and possessions, in which each person was a threat to every other; regular malicious as well as nonmalicious violations of persons' basic rights – or, perhaps, the absence of real rights altogether; the absence of justice, both procedural and substantive; and disagreement about how we ought to treat one another and when wrong has been done. Human beings thus need government and law.)

Premise 2:   All persons have a natural moral duty to (select one or more of the following):
a. Maximize goodness in the world (e.g., happiness, preference satisfaction, perfection);
b. Perform necessary tasks to which they are well suited, and support and obey those who perform necessary tasks;
c. Respect and defer to those who do necessary tasks by occupying positions of authority;
d. Do and/or promote justice;
e. Assist those in peril.

Conclusion 1: Therefore all persons have a natural moral duty to:
a. Leave the state of nature and join together with others to create government and law where none exist, and
b. Support and comply with stable existing governments and law when within their jurisdictions (Possible Proviso: provided that government and law are reasonably just).

(Explanation: Conclusion 1 is implied by the duty [or duties] in Premise 2 conjoined with a set of premises detailing the principal enduring facts about the human social condition.)

Conclusion 2:   All persons have a moral duty to obey domestic law (again with the Possible Proviso).
(Explanation: Conclusion 2 is implied by the duty in Conclusion 1 conjoined with a set of premises detailing the principal enduring facts about the human social condition.)

Consequentialism

I deal with consequentialism first only because I will say so little here about consequentialist attempts to justify a general moral duty to obey the law. If one of those attempts succeeds, of course, the argument of this essay must fail. But the strengths and weaknesses of consequentialist moral theory are not only ground that has been quite thoroughly traversed, they are properly the subject of a separate book, not of a brief section of a short essay. I try here only to note the basic reasons for my doubts that consequentialism can complete the argument in a fashion that we should find persuasive.

I understand as consequentialist any moral theory that makes the rightness or wrongness of an act depend solely on the goodness or badness of its consequences. Consequentialist theories will then differ according to the different accounts they give of the good, as well as the kinds of consequences (e.g., direct or generalized) they consider. In attempting to justify a general duty of legal obedience, consequentialist arguments will treat the necessity claim (of Premise 1) as a marker or indicator of the likely bad consequences that would result from the absence of government or law. These bad consequences might be sufficient to establish a duty not to try to overthrow an existing (reasonably just) government because of the likelihood of high transitional costs. But consequentialists need to show more than just this. They must next explain how particular acts of ordinary (i.e., nonrevolutionary) legal disobedience can be expected either to have worse direct consequences than obedience – perhaps by contributing incrementally to the extreme badness of lawlessness – or to be a worse type of action (in the circumstances) than obedience. This seems to me an explanation that cannot be convincingly given. In the following remarks, I will have in mind primarily theories that identify utility (happiness, preference satisfaction) as the good, but the claims made will apply equally to other versions of consequentialism.

Direct consequentialist arguments for legal obedience seem to me to fail today in the same way that they failed when Socrates (perhaps) advanced them: It simply seems empirically false that Socrates' escape would have either (a) had immediate bad consequences that would have outweighed the good of his survival or (b) made an interesting incremental contribution to the longer-term destruction of law and government (by contributing to a general trend of disobedience or by encouraging enough others to follow his disobedient example). More generally, while domestic legal disobedience may often have worse direct consequences than obedience, there is no guarantee that this will be the case, and we are all perfectly acquainted with the many commonplace instances in which it quite plainly is not the case. Significant personal or interpersonal good can often be done at smaller (or negligible) cost by disobeying the law (not only in the silly cases of driving through red lights at midnight in the desert, but in ordinary cases of illegal recreations, tax fraud, theft, and so on). This point is related, of course, to the more general and familiar worry that direct- or act-consequentialist theories cannot justify "secondary" principles of duty beyond the primary duty of good maximization. I have discussed these issues elsewhere[1] and will pursue them further later on as well.

It is perhaps worth noting that, historically, it was for these reasons that the utilitarian William Godwin found himself compelled to embrace a position that we would now call "anarchism." He denied (among other things) the existence of a general moral duty to obey domestic law or support one's domestic legal and

---

1 *Moral Principles and Political Obligations*, 45–54.

political institutions – no matter how many virtues they might possess – precisely because the (sole) moral duty to promote utility was inconsistent with acknowledging *any* firm secondary duties, legal and political ones included. A utilitarian must follow the demands of utility wherever they lead, even when they lead one away from domestic legal compliance.[2]

Suppose, however, that we attempt to counter such concerns about direct consequentialism by appealing instead to consequentialist generalization (of the sort that, as we have seen, Socrates may have had in mind). Unhappily for such an attempt, consequentialist generalization arguments are either utterly implausible or simply extensionally equivalent to direct consequentialist arguments.[3] Consider the dubious moral force of "what if everyone did that?" arguments.[4] Everyone's doing what I am doing right now would be a very bad thing – there would be nobody keeping the ship afloat, as it were. But it is surely not morally wrong for me to be writing a philosophical essay (or, if it is wrong, it is wrong for other reasons – such as the essay's being bad or my neglecting my family). Perhaps the idea is that I have misdescribed what I am doing right now. I am not just writing a philosophical essay, but doing so when others are busy taking care of society's (other?) necessary tasks. Everyone's doing *that* would not be bad, hence my doing so now is not wrong. But in

---

2 "In those measures which have the concurrence of my judgement [with regard to utility], I may reasonably be expected to co-operate with willingness and zeal; but, for the rest, my only justifiable ground of obedience is that I will not disturb the repose of the community, or that I do not perceive the question to be of significant magnitude to authorize me in incurring the penalty" (William Godwin, *Enquiry Concerning Political Justice* [Harmondsworth: Penguin, 1976], 239). See especially II.vi. and III.ii–vi.

3 David Lyons, *Forms and Limits of Utilitarianism* (Oxford: Oxford University Press, 1965).

4 "What if everyone did that?" arguments might sometimes have nonconsequentialist force: They might be used to show that it would be *unfair* for me to do A (pick an apple from someone else's orchard, water my lawn during a drought, etc.) when everyone else can't do A (without consequences all would regret). Where such arguments are in fact disguised fairness arguments, they qualify not as Natural Duty arguments, but rather as Transactional arguments.

that case, my disobeying the law right now would not be wrong either, since what I would be more precisely doing is disobeying the law when most others would be obeying it. And if everyone did *that*, the consequences would not be bad. The legal system (in stable societies) needs only *general* compliance to function at peak efficiency, not universal compliance. Such examples can be multiplied endlessly (what if everyone ate lunch at noon, as I am considering doing?). The general point is this: When we adjust our examples so that the consequentialist generalization arguments seem to yield plausible conclusions – by generalizing over more specifically described acts – we simply render the argument equivalent to a direct consequentialist argument, making it vulnerable to precisely the critique that consequentialist generalization was introduced to evade.

Consequentialist theories can, of course, be advanced in more sophisticated "rule-consequentialist" forms, in which they are not in this way either immediately implausible or simply equivalent to direct consequentialist arguments. But such approaches face the equally daunting problem of explaining why they should not be accused of endorsing rule-following in circumstances where it is simply irrational (from a consequentialist viewpoint) to conform one's conduct to the rule. (This is the well known "rule-worship" objection, which I believe to be conclusive.) These obstacles, along with the difficulties consequentialist theories face on the issue of particularity (discussed later in this chapter), seem to me sufficient to render unconvincing all consequentialist accounts of a duty to obey the law.

Necessity

Necessity accounts of the duty to obey offer a slightly truncated version of the argument, concentrating exclusively on the argument's necessity claims (in Premise 1) and on the supposedly direct moral implications of such "necessities" (in Premise 2.b). While necessity accounts ultimately go on to draw the same conclusion (about a duty to obey domestic law) as do other Natural Duty theories, their exclusive focus on the moral importance of need or necessity – and on the moral duties that allegedly follow immediately from claims of need/necessity, rather than on duties that follow from independent, nonnecessity-centered moral principles (such as the others identified in Premise 2) – makes these accounts appear somewhat more blunt and certainly less elaborate than their fellow family members.

The guiding idea of necessity accounts is that certain kinds of needs – in particular, needs for something or someone to be supervised or cared for or controlled – ground moral duties on suitable persons to perform the needed tasks and moral duties on others to permit and facilitate such performances. In the case at issue in this essay, the need for (institutionally acknowledged) political authorities and a stable system of law is said to ground a moral right for some to political and legal authority and a general moral duty of domestic legal compliance. Necessity claims are familiar from many areas of life, particularly in the law. Appeals to necessity in law (and in morals) generally involve using the claim of necessity either as an excuse (meaning that having done what was necessary is seen as simply not blameworthy/punishable[5]) or as a justification (so that in doing what was necessary, we are seen as having done what was actually the best/right thing to do on balance[6]).

Necessity accounts of a duty to obey the law plainly will need to regard necessity as justifying action rather than as merely excusing it. But they will further need to show how necessity claims by some can ground various moral duties on others, duties owed

---

5 Legal excuses, along with their moral analogues, include such claims as mistake or accident, duress, provocation, immaturity, or insanity. In general, the claim made is that while the action performed was not the best/right action to perform in the circumstances, the harm done was (nonnegligently) unintended or the actor was not in reasonable control of the actions (i.e., *mens rea* was absent). Punishment or blame would therefore be inappropriate.

6 A legal or moral claim of justification is a claim that an action for which one would normally be liable to punishment or blame is not, in the circumstances, one we should condemn at all. The action is, on balance, the best or right action in the circumstances. Thus, homicide, which is normally wrong, may in certain circumstances be justifiable – as when one kills another in self-defense or in defense of others.

to those who perform the necessary tasks. In many familiar cases of doing what is necessary, of course, duty seems not to be a real issue at all. Where I have no (acceptable) choice but to use deadly force in resisting your wrongful attack on me, or where I have no (acceptable) choice after the climbing accident but to cut the rope by which your heavy, unconscious body dangles below me (pulling out the anchor that supports us both), it seems odd to suppose that the necessity in question grounds moral duties on anyone. I have no obvious moral duty (at least according to many accounts of morality) to perform the necessary task – the task, in these cases, of saving myself (necessitated by our "survival instinct") – nor does anyone else have any obvious moral duty to me in consequence of my having chosen to do what is necessary. But perhaps in other kinds of cases, claims of need or necessity imply moral duties more plainly or directly. For instance, such claims may seem more persuasive in the case of necessary tasks that involve the welfare of others or in those cases that require not just momentary but ongoing action or care.

The best-known contemporary necessity account is that offered by Elizabeth Anscombe in her 1978 paper "On the Source of the Authority of the State."[7] Anscombe begins by observing that, at least in the sorts of cases relevant to our discussion here, "authority arises from the necessity of a task whose performance requires a certain sort and extent of obedience on the part of those for whom the task is supposed to be done."[8] Parental authority, for instance (to use Anscombe's example), arises from the necessity of parental care and tuition, along with the need for filial obedience in performing that task; and the child, whether she likes it or not, is bound to obey her parents simply because they are performing this necessary task. In the case of political authority

---

7 In J. Raz (ed.), *Authority* (New York: New York University Press, 1990). A similar necessity account is defended by Tony Honoré (in "Must We Obey? Necessity as a Ground of Obligation," *Virginia Law Review* 67:1 [February 1981]) and briefly discussed in Kent Greenawalt, *Conflicts of Law and Morality* (New York: Oxford University Press, 1989), 168–70.
8 Anscombe, "On the Source of the Authority of the State," 147.

and the duty to obey the law, the principal necessity in question is "a very general need of protection of life and limb against violence,"[9] and the task of meeting this need requires obedience to law. Anscombe recognizes that "the mere fact that someone is performing a task does not suffice to prove that he has a right to what is needed for the performance of the task. It must either be necessary that he should perform the task or be his right to do it, before he can derive a right to certain things from the fact that they are necessary for the performance of the task."[10] This admission, of course, might seem to threaten to render her argument redundant, since it appears to rest the authority derived from performing a necessary task on a prior right to perform it (this prior right being the interesting one). Further, in the end, Anscombe seems to have in mind that any prior right to enforce the law and demand obedience will be just a "customary right" to do so. What is supposed to make the argument work in the face of these difficulties, it seems, is a second kind of need or necessity: There is, Anscombe claims, a need that such customary rights (to make law and be obeyed) be upheld and protected. And that second need is what establishes the authority of existing states to require compliance with law.[11]

Tony Honoré's version of the necessity theory begins with the similar claim that where there is "a need for an individual, a thing, or an institution to be cared for or supervised . . . , a special duty" may fall "on the person who is deemed suitable to render this care or supervision,"[12] Like Anscombe, Honoré uses as his principal examples the moral dimensions of nonvoluntary familial relationships (which work especially well for them both, since we are naturally reluctant to challenge the moral standing of such socially central relationships, even if we cannot really explain the source of that standing): An uncle has a duty to care for his dead brother's child (where no other relatives can do so), Honoré claims; a raped mother (who could not have an abortion)

9 Ibid., 170.
10 Ibid., 161.
11 Ibid., 170–1.
12 Honoré, "Must We Obey?" 51.

has a duty to care for her unwanted child.[13] Similarly, he argues in attempting to explain the duty to obey the law, "in regard to citizens, the state and, through the state, their fellow citizens, are in a position analogous to that of an involuntary parent."[14] While this appears to suggest that the state has a duty to supervise its citizens and they have a duty to obey in order to make this supervision possible, Honoré's actual argument strays into one centered on the implied consent given by residents.[15] But so long as the theory actually concentrates on the moral significance of claims of *necessity*, it seems to have a structure similar to Anscombe's account.

I confess that after all has been said, it is still hard for me to see exactly how the necessity of a task is supposed to establish the authority to compel the compliance by others required for that task. The fact that I am ill and hungry and need care does not on its face seem to give any other person or group authority to dictate to me (and/or others, absent my and/or their consent) in whatever ways are required to meet my need. I strongly suspect that the intuitive force of Anscombe's and Honoré's claims about necessity yielding moral authority and moral duty depends heavily on the nature of the specific examples they employ, all of which, remember, concern family relationships. In these cases, I think, we simply *assume* (perhaps without realizing it) an unstated, heavily conventional background morality of family relationships. We do not *derive* this morality from morally neutral facts about the necessity of certain tasks. The intuitive force of the claims made about the authority and duties of parents and uncles draws not on the nonmoral necessity of *those* people doing *those* tasks, but rather simply on our prior conviction that parents and family members do in fact have special moral rights and duties with respect to one another.

But suppose that we grant, *arguendo*, that nonmoral necessity/need does in fact, at least in some cases, ground morally

13 Ibid., 52.
14 Ibid., 56.
15 See David Lyons' reconstruction of Honoré's argument in "Need, Necessity, and Political Obligation," *Virginia Law Review* 67:1 (February 1981), esp. 73–5.

legitimate claims to authority and genuine moral duties of compliance. Even granting this starting point of necessity theories, questions about whether the theory can actually yield a moral duty to obey domestic law abound. There are at least four general aspects of necessity arguments that need to be examined and questioned:

(i) Exactly what makes a task necessary? There is, in my view, no such thing as (nonmoral, nonlogical) necessity *simpliciter*. Tasks are necessary only for or relative to some purpose, end, or desire. Necessity claims in law, for instance, typically concern not what literally must be done, but rather what must be done if certain valuable and valued ends (e.g., life, security, health) are to be secured. Self-defense is not literally necessary unless one assumes that it is necessary to pursue the end of survival (which, of course, it is not). Parents and uncles do not *need* to care for the young children in their families, though we believe they should. Children could simply be allowed to die from lack of care, or they could live and prosper as a result of care provided by nonrelatives. Family members' caring for children is only necessary provided that (a) others are unlikely to provide that care (because of social convention, indifference, etc.), and (more importantly) (b) the goals of children's survival and well-being are goals that are themselves necessary for us – that is, they are goals we are morally required to pursue, goals to which we are strongly personally committed, or goals we otherwise find irresistible. So the persuasiveness of necessity claims to authority and compliance will turn crucially on whether we share the goals or ends relative to which tasks are said to be necessary, or on how we evaluate the importance of these goals or ends. Necessity claims are at best a convenient (and illicitly forceful?) shorthand for claims about the value or importance of certain tasks.

And related concerns can, of course, be raised concerning the ideas, utilized in necessity theories, of certain persons being "suitable" for particular tasks – what exactly is it that makes an uncle suitable for caring for his dead brother's child, beyond our *prior* conviction that uncles ought morally to take on such tasks? – and of things being "required" for the performance of the necessary tasks – is filial obedience really *required* for parents to care for their children, or does it just make the task much easier and more palatable? I will address these concerns in (ii)–(iv). Perhaps in the end, though, many readers will still share the necessity theorist's convictions about the nature and source of parental authority and filial duty.

It will be harder, I believe, for necessity theorists to convince those readers about the (supposedly analogous) cases of political authority and citizens' duty to obey the law. For in this case the claims that have to be made about the necessity of the task, the suitability of the authority holder, and the things required for the performance of the task are all far more contentious. Taking first the necessity of the task, political and legal institutions (and the tasks that they, as a class, perform) have, of course, often been taken as necessities. Hobbes famously claimed that they were necessary to keep all of our lives from being "solitary, poor, nasty, brutish, and short"; for without the state (or "sovereign") to forbid violence and dishonesty and to threaten punishment for noncompliance, there are too many powerful motives in persons that will inevitably produce war and misery. States allow the provision of security and coordination as public goods. Indeed, without states, the argument goes, a wide variety of important public goods simply would not be produced. Virtually all of us, of course, would strongly prefer that our lives be social, rich, pleasant, cultured, and long; so we will certainly be inclined to agree with Hobbes that if politics and law, political authority and legal obedience, are in fact necessary for avoiding a short, unhappy life, politics and law are very good things.

Now the facts at issue in this claim have frequently been challenged. Anarchists, for instance, have often argued that not only are the legal and political institutions of the state not necessary for us all to lead decent lives, these institutions are themselves the cause of most of the antisocial motives that are alleged to make the institutions necessary in the first place. Others (including some "philosophical anarchists," like myself) have maintained that life under political and legal institutions has certain obvious costs (in individual autonomy, for example), and that persons are not obliged to favor the package of costs and benefits provided by the state over the package that could be had without the state. The tasks the state performs are necessary only in the sense of being highly valued by most, even when the costs attached to receiving the benefits of the state are factored in. Whether or not one shares in this general valuation is a matter for each individual. So even if necessity claims *are* capable of justifying authority and a duty to obey, the state's authority (and the citizen's duty to obey) would still have to be taken to vary according to these individual valuations. The authority and duty to obey authority could not be perfectly general. If necessity claims do not by themselves justify authority, of course, then people who value what is necessary are still free to choose it, opting for the subjection to legal duty that this involves. Those who do not are morally free to opt out. But that would mean that the duty to obey must in fact be understood in a transactional way. Either way, a necessity that is only relative to certain standard desires or ends can get us only this far.

These arguments seem to me to be not without merit. But let us allow for now that the challenges of life without law and the state are more or less as Hobbes believed them to be, and that we all agree in preferring life in a state to life without. What, exactly, should we take to follow from such an admission? The necessity theorist would have us infer from it that some suitable person or group (or set of institutions?) thereby has the authority to perform the necessary tasks (i.e., the ones that states perform), and that all others whose actions can affect this performance thereby have a moral duty to do what is required to permit the performance of these tasks. The real-life applications of the argument are supposed to be these: The required conduct in question is obedience to domestic law by all citizens (and some others[16]); and

---

16 This group would include, of course, visitors and resident aliens within the law's jurisdiction. The logic of the argument suggests, however, that it might include as well anybody anywhere who could by his or her actions interfere with the completion of the necessary tasks. So the argument would appear to have as its conclusion not only a moral duty to obey domestic law, but a far broader moral duty binding all persons to act as required by the performance of the task.

the suitable person or group with authority is simply our existing set of domestic political and legal officials (or institutions?). But none of this follows as simply as it might at first blush appear to.

(ii) What is required for the performance of a necessary task? Can we actually derive a moral duty to obey from such an idea of requirement? (If a kidney is required for my survival, and so is needed or necessary, do all suitable donors have a clear moral duty to provide one?) All children disobey their parents, some quite regularly. Yet parents still seem to succeed in a perhaps surprising number of cases in raising reasonably (or at least acceptably) well-adjusted children, despite the parents' own frequent poor judgment and despite circumstances often involving financial difficulties, marital and emotional stress, and so on. In what sense, then, is filial obedience required for completion of the necessary task, rather than just being very helpful or convenient to its completion? Are the helpfulness or convenience of actions by others sufficient to ground a moral duty so to act? If it would be very helpful to me in the task of raising my child (but not strictly required for it) that others regularly watch over and help pay the expenses incurred in caring for my child, do they have a moral duty to contribute in these ways? In any event, children do not, I think (for a variety of reasons), generally have a moral duty to obey their parents, nor could such a duty be derived from considerations of necessity and requirement if all other arguments for such a conclusion failed (as I believe they do[17]).

The argument from necessity (and from what is required for the necessary task) works, if anything, even less well in the case of trying to derive a general moral duty of domestic legal compliance. Grant, as we have done, the necessity of the task (of guaranteeing peace and security, providing public goods, and so on, through the operation of a formal legal system). But what, exactly, is required for the completion of this task, as opposed to merely very helpful or convenient to its completion? As I will urge in greater detail, universal compliance with legal requirements is

17 See my discussion of filial duties of obedience in *The Lockean Theory of Rights* (Princeton, NJ: Princeton University Press, 1992), section 4.2.

not required for performing the necessary tasks done by our political and legal institutions and officials (however those tasks might be enumerated or characterized). Legal systems tolerate quite impressive levels of noncompliance without performing the tasks in question interestingly less well (than they would with greater compliance). Universal legal obedience might well be helpful or convenient to performance of the tasks of a legal system, but it is plainly not required. Disobedience by some, while most others are obeying, seems unlikely to impede performance of the necessary task. Further, of course, we all confront reasonably regularly circumstances in which it will simply make no difference to anything whether we obey or disobey the law. So it is hard to see how the idea of obedience being required for the necessary tasks of the state can really justify our extending the state's authority – and our moral duty to obey – to those frequent instances in which compliance with authoritative commands simply is not in any recognizable sense required for the accomplishment of whatever might be identified as the state's necessary tasks.

Similar conclusions follow from the simple observation that typical states perform many functions that are completely unrelated to their performance of the necessary tasks of guaranteeing peace and security. While (for example) interstate highways, national parks, and national museums may all be things that we want our states to provide, the coercive collection of tax dollars required for their provision can hardly be justified by appeal to the necessity of the task. These goods are simply not necessary in anything like the sense in which basic security is necessary. But if that is true, then an argument from the necessity of the state could at best ground a duty of very partial obedience to law, with obedience (e.g., to tax laws) being required only insofar as obedience was supporting the state's genuinely necessary activities.

(iii) On precisely whom does necessity confer authority? Even supposing that necessity theories of the duty to obey could establish that institutional authority and general compliance are essential to accomplishing certain necessary tasks, it would still remain insufficiently clear why the relevant authority should be located in one party rather than another. Why should biological parents (or other blood relatives) be thought to be the ones on whom the authority to perform the task of childrearing principally falls? Any notion of natural suitability for a task – that is, any notion of suitability that is not itself thoroughly and illicitly loaded with conventional and moral content – will plainly not do the job here. Blood relatives are often quite thoroughly unsuited to the tasks in question, especially – but certainly not exclusively – where the children are unwanted or are not the direct offspring of the blood caregiver. While biological parents often love and feel naturally bound to their offspring, this is certainly not always the case; and one who is in fact unrelated to a child by blood may often feel rather more strongly about that child's well-being than do its blood relatives. The authority of biological parents over their offspring (and that of other blood relatives, as next in line) is quite plainly customary, based at best only in extremely broad (and regularly contradicted) generalities about natural suitability.

All that I have said of parental authority is, one might think, even more true in the case of domestic political and legal authorities. While the administration currently in power normally enjoys customary (and legal) rights to be the group that makes and enforces law (and so on), we would be hard pressed to argue that these rights arise from their natural suitability to the task. Lawmakers often are (and have in the past normally been) either inheritors of their positions or brutal conquerors, neither of which source of authority seems likely to track natural suitability for peaceful rule. And even elected lawmakers are certainly not uniformly (and, the more cynical might say, are virtually never) those best suited to the necessary tasks at hand (as opposed, say, to being those best suited to the rather different tasks of fundraising, campaigning, spouting empty rhetoric, and projecting attractive images). Why, then, should we take such customary assignments of political and legal authority to signify anything of moral interest? More to the point, why should a necessity theorist see them as morally interesting if they track so poorly natural suitability for the relevant necessary tasks?

The only reply that I can locate in defenses of (or think of to help) the necessity theory is Anscombe's: The kinds of customary rights to authority in question here – those of biological parents and those of officials lawfully in power – are themselves needed, and so are themselves morally justified by their necessity. But should we be persuaded by such a response even if we are sympathetic to claims about the moral implications of necessity? It may well be that *some* customary distribution of authority is necessary if all is not simply to be left to the control of the strongest or the most persuasive. And it may well be, in addition, that the distribution of customary rights in question is better or more useful than would be other patterns of distribution that we can easily imagine: Giving authority to those most likely to care about the children needing to be raised is clearly superior to distributing parental authority randomly among all adults, say; allowing political and legal authority to go to those who are elected for it or to those who inherit it seems better than letting it go to those who seize it by force or who make the highest bid for it (the latter of which, those cynics might note, is perilously close to the actual rule in existing democracies). But the fact that the accepted range of customary rights to authority seems better than others that we can imagine does not show that the customary distribution of authority is somehow necessary or even beyond moral criticism. And if it does not show this, then why (from the point of view of necessity theory) are the customary assignments of authority not morally open to challenge from those who disagree with them – especially from those who correctly contend that they could perform the necessary task in question better than the person or group to which customary rights assign authority to act?

Consider for the moment the moral position of rival claimants to the authority assigned by customary right to officials lawfully in power. Why should rival claims to authority to perform a necessary task be thought to be automatically inferior to the claims of those in power? Being in power may or may not indicate superior ability, understanding, or, more generally, possession in greater measure of those traits that facilitate performance of the necessary tasks. Displacing those who are in power and on the job routinely will, of course, introduce various transaction costs that would not have to be paid by allowing them to remain in power.

But the same is plainly true of displacing clearly illegitimate officials, and we do not regard the costs of transferring power in those cases as necessarily undermining purported justifications for removing and replacing the illegitimate officials who are currently in place. As in that case, the moral defensibility of rival claims to authority seems to turn less on who currently holds what than it does on whose claim to authority is more justifiable in the relevant terms. Where the relevant terms are necessity, rival claims to authority seem likely to be sometimes capable of being very well justified.

I will not try to examine carefully here the claims to parental authority of biological parents, as these might be compared to possible rival claims by others. Much of the force of biological parents' (apparently superior) claims turns, in my view, on shared intuitions about property (in the child) and labor (by the mother), neither of which has any obvious relevance to the supposedly analogous case of the political authority of those who make and administer law. Perhaps we should suppose that the analogy between the two cases consists in the fact that both biological parents and existing political authorities are "first come" to the necessary tasks, and so should both be "first served." The superiority of their claims to authority over those of their rival claimants lies simply in their having gotten there first.

But this defense seems implausible. "First come, first served" is a maxim that appears to track the moral superiority of claims principally in cases where equal opportunities remain for others to make similar claims on different portions. Thus, for instance, Locke can plausibly argue that the first person to labor productively on unowned nature acquires a special claim (i.e., private property) in it, but only because he adds that others must be left "enough and as good" on which to make similar claims of their own.[18] Political authority, however, is by definition exclusive and monopolistic. Your first claim on such authority leaves nothing else to be claimed by rival domestic claimants. It is a case not of first come, first served, but rather of first come, only one served.

18 John Locke, *Second Treatise of Government*, section 27.

Why should we believe that the necessity of the tasks of making and enforcing laws implies that those first on the job have the only legitimate claim to be the ones to perform those tasks? On its face, the logic of the necessity argument seems to drive us in the direction of assigning authority to those who will do the necessary task best (most efficiently, justly, etc.), not to those who happen to be doing it now. In order to defend a conservative account of the *location* of the authority to perform necessary tasks (as opposed to just defending the *need* for such authority), necessity theorists seem compelled to appeal to nonnecessity considerations – considerations of the sort that we will consider in the subsequent sections of this chapter.

(iv) Finally, on precisely whom does necessity impose duties? We have considered necessity theory's claims about the location of authority, but have not thus far pressed that theory on the question of the location of the moral duties that theory wishes to assign to others to facilitate the tasks performed by the authorities. Since these duties – and, particularly, the moral duty to obey the law – are our primary concern in this essay and will be discussed extensively in the remainder, I will here say enough only to introduce what I take to be two classes of persons that should be particularly troublesome for necessity theory (and, indeed, as we will see, for all Natural Duty theories). The classes of persons I have in mind we can call "unusual valuers" and "self-providers." Government and law are said by necessity theories to perform a variety of necessary tasks. Others are said to owe moral duties to obey (and otherwise facilitate performance of the tasks by) the established authorities. What shall we say, though, of those who simply disagree with the necessity claim, not sharing the preferences or values (or the weighting of these preferences or values) of that majority for whom the goods provided by the state are indeed necessities (perhaps because they value more greatly than the majority such goods as independence, autonomy, and self-government)?[19] And what shall we say of persons or groups that

---

19 I speak here of conflicting values or preferences not because I believe (with some consequentialists) that it is the job of the state to somehow resolve

strongly prefer to provide for themselves, where possible, those benefits that law and government supply, and to simply do without where self-provision is impossible? Self-providers want to do their best, say, to provide security for themselves (with vigilance, defenses, or hired guards), to interact economically with others without outside guidance or control, to make and maintain with others roads and common spaces, to self-provide for emergencies, and so on. How does the necessity of a task speak to those who want to do the task (insofar as they even accept its necessity) themselves? Provided that they interact peacefully with others, they seem not to endanger the performance by others of the tasks those others take to be necessary. Yet we know, of course, that self-provision is routinely prohibited and punished by the authorities of existing political communities, and that the moral duty to obey the law is normally taken to bind all within the relevant legal jurisdiction, regardless of whether (or how much) they value the goods secured for all by law. Do unusual valuers and would-be self-providers have a moral duty to obey the law, along with all the others who are subject to domestic law? It is not clear how simple considerations of necessity can help us to answer this question in the affirmative, as necessity theorists purport to be able to do. In this way too, then, necessity theory appears to lack the resources to explain a general moral duty to obey the law.

In the end, then, necessity theories look more like the first stage of an account of our duty to obey the law than a complete account (just as the structure of "the argument" suggests). The natural ways to try to complete the argument for a duty to obey involve first appealing to the kinds of nonnecessity-based natural moral duties noted in Premise 2 of the argument. Theories that incorporate such duties seem better positioned to respond effectively to my four concerns about simple necessity theories. Whether or not the more complicated theories utilizing these natural duties

such conflicts or to aggregate preferences. Rather, I intend this point about the possibility of unusual values or preferences to speak only to the kinds of claims of need or necessity made in necessity theories of a duty to obey. I take individuals' values and preferences to regularly bear heavily on what is necessary for (or needed by) them.

can actually overcome these obstacles to a plausible account of the duty to obey will be the question asked in the remaining parts of this chapter.

Respect and Deference

Suppose, then, that we agree that necessity theories are importantly incomplete as accounts of a general moral duty to obey domestic law. How might the argument be more satisfactorily continued to yield the desired conclusion? In her defense of the necessity theory of authority, Anscombe observed in passing that "authority might be thought to be a right to decide in some domain, and its correlate not to be obedience, but respect."[20] Respect, one might naturally believe, is in fact a key issue in addressing the question of how we ought to relate to our political and legal superiors. After all, those who defy and make light of the authorities are often criticized as being disrespectful. And respect is something that most of us believe we owe to others, at least insofar as they are making a good-faith effort to do what they believe is right (and perhaps even when they are not). Indeed, the point might be not so much that we should focus on respect *rather than* obedience, as Anscombe's remark suggests, but rather that respect and obedience are importantly related, so that the moral importance of respecting others might be a fruitful starting place for trying to understand a moral duty to obey. And emphasizing the importance of respect, of course, will develop more obviously the Kantian character of the argument. While Kant was certainly moved by aspects of the simple necessity argument, he was much more centrally concerned with the moral imperative that we respect one another (that is, that we treat one another as ends in ourselves). As we will see, however, the Kantian's insistence on mutual respect (as an aspect of an argument for a duty to obey) can take many forms.

Philip Soper has recently defended a Kantian natural duty theory that relies on the importance of respect in a particularly

<hr>

20 Anscombe, "On the Source of the Authority of the State," 148.

straightforward way. In some of his earlier work, Soper's claims mirrored closely those made in the argument.[21] The necessity of coercive government being established, persons who make a good-faith effort to do what is necessary – by governing, by making and enforcing law – are owed respect for this effort by those who find themselves subject to political and legal authority. Showing respect for others importantly includes taking seriously what those others care about (Soper again uses the family analogy, comparing the position of citizens with that of the child who owes respect to her parents); and political and legal officials act in the hope and expectation that others will voluntarily comply with the laws they make and enforce. Legal disobedience, then, shows disrespect for those officials (just as filial disobedience shows disrespect for parents who are making good-faith efforts to do an important job), breaching (what we might call) the natural duty of respect.

Soper's most recent work, *The Ethics of Deference*, revises, extends, and explains his earlier defense of a duty of legal compliance, utilizing a wide-ranging and interesting exploration of the moral importance of deference to others. It is on this more recent and complete account that I will concentrate here. According to Soper, many of the familiar philosophical puzzles about obligation and obedience can best be addressed and solved through attention to (what he calls) the "ethics of deference." Persons may, he claims, often have strong moral reasons (including moral obligations or duties) "to defer to the views of others, including the state, in deciding what to do . . . – even if the views to which they defer are wrong."[22] Such occasions include when those persons have made promises to others, when community norms require them to cooperate in producing important collective goods, and when persons are required to act or forbear by domestic law. The obligation to keep promises, obligations of fair play, and political

---

21 See especially *A Theory of Law* (Cambridge, MA: Harvard University Press, 1984) and "Another Look at the *Crito*," *American Journal of Jurisprudence* 41 (1996).

22 *The Ethics of Deference*, 8. Subsequent references to the book in this section will be in parentheses in the text.

obligation (including the duty to obey the law) are all, then, to be explained similarly by reference to the idea of moral reasons for deference. In this respect, Soper's approach to explaining the duty to obey is importantly like Hume's (as Soper notes [28]), since both, rather than trying to derive that duty from a more fundamental one, instead argue that the duty to obey stands on precisely the same footing as (and is equally as basic as) the duties from which other theorists have tried to derive it.

Promises, Soper argues, should be kept not only for the familiar utilitarian reasons (that apply in many cases), and because deference to the wishes of the promisee is sometimes (as in reasonably intimate contexts) necessary for the promiser to show respect for others, but because the clearest point to the practice of promising (a point that almost all persons recognize and accept) is precisely to assign to the promisee the right to decide (and to the promiser the obligation to defer) in cases where the parties disagree about what ought to be done (136–8). Duties of fair play, on Soper's view, similarly "ultimately depend on the obligation to respect the views of others, even where those views differ from our own." Where a norm requiring deference (i.e., playing one's expected part in the scheme) is in place in the relevant community, and where "valuable goods are at stake," persons have moral duties to "play fair" and do their part (157–8).

Political obligation (and the duty to obey domestic law) requires a defense that is slightly different than the ones Soper offers for promissory and fair play duties. But because the duty to obey the law is precisely a duty to obey even when one disagrees with the law, this duty too, he argues, is best understood as a moral duty to defer to the views of others. "The respect shown by deference in [this case] is required not solely or even primarily because of the consequences if one fails to defer" (163); "no single act of disobedience is likely to have significant effects on the community" (164). Rather, "the reasons for deference in the case of law are Kantian in character, demanding that one avoid . . . inconsistency between one's actions and one's own admitted norms." The state (with its legal system) is necessary (for security) and "is the kind of entity that requires some to govern, in good faith, on behalf of all" (167). Unless I am a sincere anarchist who denies this, "the law's expectation of voluntary compliance corresponds to what I would expect if I were the legislator. The duty to respect the legal norm is a reflection of the duty to respect the values I myself acknowledge" (164). So legal disobedience both "shows disrespect for hypothetical others (legislators who [may not] know but whose expectations are clear), as well as for one's own values" (172). "Understanding what a legal system is *and admitting that it is valuable*" entails "that one is being *morally* inconsistent in denying that deference is due to the state's norms" (173; emphasis in the original).

I am frankly uncertain what to make of the idea of disrespect to "hypothetical others." But legal disobedience, I think, just cannot be taken (in normal circumstances) to show morally wrong disrespect to *actual* legislators, regardless of the facts of legislators' alleged good-faith efforts to do a necessary task and their alleged expectations of compliance. In the first place, legislators' motives and expectations are normally both deeply mixed and (partly in consequence) unclear to citizens, making consciously disrespectful conduct quite a difficult enterprise; and, unless they are fools, legislators' expectations certainly do not include universal voluntary compliance with law by the citizenry. Further, the fact that I myself would want others to obey my laws, were I a legislator, seems no more relevant to my present duties than does the fact that I would want others to buy my product were I a manufacturer. Unless the necessity of the task by itself suffices to ground particular rights and obligations – as we have already seen that it does not – the obvious difference between legislating and manufacturing appears not to be a relevant difference for the force of an argument from "hypothetical desire." If necessity arguments cannot by themselves establish the location of authority and a general duty to obey it, how can the mere fact that were I in power I would want my authority respected make any difference to the conclusion?

More importantly, however, the idea of showing respect for another (or oneself) is notoriously obscure. And there are many kinds and degrees of disrespect, not all of which are morally wrong. Does a child's playing hooky really show morally prohibited disrespect for his teachers and school administration (who do a necessary task and expect his attendance)? If so, it does so in a *very* different way than would his assaulting them, ridiculing them in public, or actively obstructing their efforts to educate willing students. It may or may not frustrate their expectations or even their desires. One thing it surely does *not* do is demonstrate disrespect for them in any very *clear* or obviously morally prohibited fashion. When one of my undergraduate students calls me "dude," his fellow students might say that he is "dissing" me. He is failing to demonstrate appropriate awe in an encounter with someone of my lofty status. But he is plainly breaching no moral duty. We can call disrespectful actions ranging from independent-minded unconventionality and simple impoliteness all the way to violent assault. And the disrespectful acts at either end of this spectrum have, I think, very little in common from the moral perspective.

Disrespect in the Kantian (and morally serious) sense, in my view, essentially concerns failing to treat others as autonomous sources of value (as ends in themselves), treating them solely as means to our own ends. We can do this by killing them, by disabling them or in other ways interfering with their autonomous pursuits, by failing to give help that is necessary to their capacity for autonomous action, and so on. It is these kinds of actions (or omissions) that are forbidden by our natural moral duties, the proscriptions and requirements at issue being plainly necessary to mutually respectful and civil coexistence. But mere disobedience to rules made by others and applied by them to us (without our consent or participation), particularly where such disobedience does not directly compromise, frustrate, or adversely affect their enterprises, seems unlikely to qualify as obviously disrespectful to others in any very strong, morally important sense. As a result, having (correctly, in my view) conceded that legal disobedience often has no real effect on the community or its legal system (or its legislators), Soper will have a very difficult time persuading us that legal disobedience nonetheless typically demonstrates the kind of serious disrespect for others that is forbidden by our natural moral duties.

What, though, of the other part – apparently now the central part – of Soper's argument for a moral duty to obey? He argues, remember, that in disobeying the law we are inconsistent with our own values/norms, provided only that we (as nonanarchists [or, in my case, as only a philosophical anarchist]) are prepared to concede that the legal system has value. Soper also assumes, of course, that we do, as Kant seemed to insist, have a moral duty to avoid such inconsistency. But we can certainly question Soper's belief that mere moral inconsistency of this sort is morally prohibited. The death squad member, sincerely affirming the value of the program of ethnic cleansing in which he is engaged, clearly does no moral wrong in letting some of his intended victims escape (whether on a whim, out of sudden squeamishness, or from some remaining shred of simple humanity). Inconsistency with one's sincerely affirmed values seems to me to bear far more directly on questions of personal integrity (which is, as this example illustrates, not always even a moral virtue[23]) than it does on the question of our moral duties. So it seems reasonable to question the very starting point of this portion of Soper's argument, however familiar it may be to us from discussions of Kantian ethics.

More important for our purposes here, however, are the questions that ought to be raised about the rest of Soper's argument – and, in particular, about his claims concerning the implications of sincere ascriptions of value. Understanding something and admitting that it has value, Soper appears to contend, entails accepting certain moral duties to uphold or promote that thing (and thus the values it embodies). But accepting moral duties (in the sense of believing that I have them) is clearly not the same as actually having those duties. And even the lesser claim – that admitting value entails accepting duties – seems clearly false. Indeed, it seems false even when we are talking about the performance of those necessary tasks that Soper clearly has chiefly in mind. I can understand the warlord's position of power and admit that

---

23 For a convincing defense of this view, see Nancy Schauber, "Integrity, Commitment, and the Concept of a Person," *American Philosophical Quarterly* 33:1 (January 1996).

his rule has value (he ruthlessly suppresses theft and murder, say, taking on that necessary task) without being in any way committed to (or bound by) a moral duty to support his position or obey his rules. What matters in such cases is surely whether I take (or take correctly) the power he exercises in his dealings with me (and others) to be legitimately exercised. And that issue cannot (as we have seen) be addressed by simply observing that he seized the power first.[24]

The point I am making here can perhaps be better formulated in terms of the distinction I have drawn between (what I have called) the "justification" of some institutional (or other) arrangement and its "legitimacy" with respect to me.[25] We can justify arrangements simply by demonstrating that their existence is a good thing, that we have good reason to create or refrain from destroying such things. We justify them by showing that arrangements have value, that their benefits outweigh their costs, that they possess interesting virtues. By contrast, legitimating an arrangement that involves some claiming the authority to control others involves showing that a special relationship of a morally weighty kind exists between those persons, such that those particular persons should have authority and those particular others should have a duty to respect that authority. This kind of legitimation simply cannot be demonstrated by merely pointing to the justifying virtues of an arrangement; a different kind of argument is required. There are (and have been) many good arrangements (e.g., many schemes for producing worthwhile public goods) that have withered or disappeared precisely because they

---

24 Soper acknowledges his acceptance in many cases of what seems to be "normative power for 'whoever goes first'," attempting to justify this counterintuitive principle by claiming that it is not really going first that matters, so much as that once another has gone first, my refusal to defer will result in an inferior sort of community (e.g., a competitive one) between us (ibid., 174, 179). But because Soper acknowledges that legal disobedience (i.e., nondeference to legal authorities) will often have no effects at all on the community, this rationale for deferring (which seems to me weak even in the most favorable cases) simply cannot apply to the case of legal and political authority – the case with which we (and apparently Soper) are most concerned.

25 See my "Justification and Legitimacy," especially 123–30, 135–9, 154–5.

could not plausibly claim the authority to require that persons support them. That an arrangement is a good thing plainly cannot give persons authority over simply whomever they might choose to select as subjects. Only a legitimating special relationship, not a justifying virtue or benefit, can ground claims of authority and subjection. Control of some by others is personal; so must be its legitimation. The impersonal virtues of arrangements involving control simply do not entail personal legitimations of control.

Where we harm or threaten harm to no others, control of us by others without our consent constitutes a clear limitation of our autonomous pursuit of value – a limitation in the name of values that we may not share or rate highly. In some cases, limiting our freedom is plainly necessary in order to compel respect for the similar freedom of others (though precisely who is entitled to do this limiting remains an issue). But where this is not the case – that is, where we harm or threaten harm to no others' autonomous pursuit of values – any argument purporting to demonstrate a moral duty on us to defer to others or to obey rules made by them for us will always look suspiciously like a mere rationalization of their desire to get their way, by forcing us to do what they want us to, without any justification that we could reasonably be expected to accept. While the desire is understandable, it is not defensible. Where controlling me is not necessary for respecting another's autonomy, respecting *me* requires that my wishes and will be taken seriously.

This is the point of the traditional (voluntarist) insistence that the legitimation of my subjection to practices and rules made by others requires my voluntary agreement. This is why consent theory retains its strong appeal, for both theorists and ordinary persons, despite its (inevitable) historical failure to demonstrate the existence of those widespread political obligations (and duties to obey the law) in which so many people seem to believe. The subjection of some to the will of others is a serious matter, morally speaking, and its defense requires powerful moral argument. Those who subject others without such defense do so at their own hazard (both prudentially and morally). Soper, of course, denies this. In arguing that promissory obligations and the duty to obey the law are equally basic, requiring similar justifications in terms of the ethics of deference, Soper tries to deny that the obvious difference between the two – that is, that promissory obligations must be undertaken voluntarily, where the duty to obey falls willy nilly on all in the state's territories – is a relevant difference. But his ultimate defense of this view is only that "legal systems are necessary in a way that making promises is not."[26] And we have seen that such claims of necessity will not save the day in attempts to demonstrate either the existence or the location of authority or particular duties to respect authority.

The Natural Duty of Justice

Doing Justice

It may seem that my critique of Soper can appear to succeed only because it unfairly fails to explore deeply enough the ways in which refusal to acknowledge a moral duty to obey domestic law shows disrespect for (and a failure of obligatory deference to) others. We can see this, it might be thought, simply by reviewing the well-known arguments to that conclusion mounted by the most important of the Kantian Natural Duty theorists, namely, Kant himself. The respect at issue in Kant's own arguments seems not to be the respect that we owe to legal officials making good-faith efforts to do a necessary task (or to be based in what we ourselves would want or expect were we such officials). Rather, according to Kant, we fail to respect others simply by living near them without an institutional enforcement of justice, for in doing so we threaten them with unjust conduct. Respect for others requires that we not so threaten them. One who lives near me "in a mere state of nature robs me of any . . . security and injures me by virtue of this very state in which he coexists with me. He may not have injured me actively . . . , but he does injure me by the very lawlessness of his state . . . , for he is a permanent threat to me."[27]

---

26 Soper, *The Ethics of Deference*, 164. See also 110–11.
27 Kant, *Political Writings*, ed. H. Reiss, trans. H. B. Nisbet (Cambridge: Cambridge University Press, 1991), 98n.

Kant also makes this same point in the language of justice.[28] As a consequence, for Kant, justice (or right) requires that we (where necessary) create and on all occasions submit to (i.e., obey and support) the legal and political institutions charged with doing justice in our societies.[29]

Suppose, then, that we begin by understanding the Kantian claim as follows: Our duty to obey our countries' laws can be derived from a more general natural moral duty to do or promote justice. One might, of course, understand a natural duty of justice in any of a variety of ways, given the many ways in which we (along with moral, legal, and political philosophers) have used the term "justice." But undoubtedly the most basic and fundamental meaning given to the term is simply respect for or satisfaction of the moral rights of others. This is Kant's understanding of justice as well: The duties of justice (duties of right, juridical duties) are the perfect duties that we owe to others – that is, the duties that correlate with others' rights.[30] We do or promote justice when we discharge our duty not to personally violate others' rights and/or our more comprehensive duty to help ensure that others' rights are not violated by anyone (i.e., that all get that to which they have moral rights, that all are treated justly). The derivation of a duty to obey the law proceeds, then, by arguing that discharging this duty (to respect the rights of others) requires, in part, that we obey the laws in force over the territories in which we reside, as well perhaps as those in force where we visit (provided, at least, that the laws themselves are tolerably just).

In its most minimal form, the natural duty of justice would require only that we refrain from personally violating others' rights

---

28 Ibid., 137–8, 165.
29 "And I can require him either to enter into a common lawful state along with me or to move away from my vicinity" (ibid., 98n). Kant's own arguments actually focus on what is necessary for individuals to be secure in their enjoyment of their rights specifically to acquire and possess things – that is, *property*. This emphasis on property rights in things – as opposed to other kinds of rights to liberty and nonaggression – is not shared by contemporary Kantians, and I will ignore it here.
30 Kant, *The Metaphysics of Morals*, trans. M. Gregor (Cambridge: Cambridge University Press, 1991), 47, 64–5.

(rather than also assisting in minimizing rights violations by anyone). Those rights might be purely negative (rights to forebearances only), so that we do justice when we refrain from aggression toward or breaking faith with others. Or the rights in question might include positive rights (rights that we act positively for others' benefit), such as rights of rescue or charity, held by the needy against those who are in a position to help. Locke is probably the best-known classical philosopher who employs this latter version of the minimal conception of a duty of justice. For Locke, the rights we must not violate in order to do justice include both negative and positive rights; he clearly defends not only the familiar rights against aggression by others, but also (contrary to his popular reputation) a right to charity – that is, a right to the surplus goods of others where receiving those goods is necessary to one's survival.[31] The same minimal conception of justice – where justice requires only personal restraint – is embraced by many contemporary libertarians, though they often decline to include general positive rights in their list of others' moral claims against us.[32]

What is distinctive about this minimal conception of the natural duty of justice is that, so conceived, the duty can plainly be discharged by individuals regardless of their social circumstances. Even in a relatively disorganized state of nature (as Locke emphasizes) it is perfectly possible – even if sometimes difficult – for persons to do their duty, obeying the natural law requirement of respect for others' rights. In peaceful social – but nonpolitical – settings, doing justice would presumably be easier, while in a legally ordered contemporary political society, it seems, it would be easier still. But if the duty of justice could be discharged in a nonpolitical social condition, then it is hard to see how we could reasonably derive from the duty of justice a duty to obey our countries' laws. If the duty in question can be fully discharged by persons in conditions where there is no law, it is

---

31 For an extended discussion of this positive side of Locke's theory of rights, see my *The Lockean Theory of Rights*, Chapter 6.
32 The standard libertarian view of positive moral rights appears to be that these can arise only from promise (contract, consent) or deliberate or negligent injury (requiring rectification/reparation).

difficult to see why it could not be fully discharged by performing those same actions in conditions that include a functioning legal system. While performing these actions might in fact regularly satisfy the legal system's requirements – since the rules of most legal systems at least overlap the rules of morality, forbidding actions like rape and murder that also violate people's moral rights – there would be no general duty to obey the law. Our duty would be only to respect the moral rights of others, whether or not doing so satisfied the demands of law. Only if people's basic moral rights were somehow altered by their being born within a political society with a legal system would a duty to obey the law seem to follow naturally from a duty of justice.

It is, however, relatively easy to see how a duty to obey the law might be believed to flow from the natural duty of justice if we understand justice or the rights of others in a slightly more expansive – but still perfectly familiar – fashion. For instance, it is common to think of justice in a way that involves a certain distribution of social goods, including income and wealth. Justice, we might argue, requires a much more equal division of wealth than is currently in evidence in the world (or in one's own country) in order that none be left dependent on the largesse of others and so that all enjoy a guaranteed level of material well-being sufficient for a decent life and the pursuit of rewarding plans or projects. All persons, we might continue, have a moral right, held against all others, that such distributive goals be achieved. Thus, the failure to achieve them in fact constitutes an injustice in our original sense – namely, a violation of others' rights.

Understanding others' rights – and the duty of justice – in this broader fashion has one clear consequence that is directly relevant to our current concerns about a duty to obey the law. Where persons are conceived of as enjoying rights (held against us) to a certain "distributive condition," we can no longer argue that the duty to respect others' rights can be easily discharged by individuals in a chaotic state of nature or in any other kind of nonpolitical setting. For only the most bizarre good fortune could ever put an individual in a situation where he was able to unilaterally completely restructure and subsequently maintain the proper distribution of property in the world (or even in his society, if we think of the duty as owed only more locally). Similarly, it would take a very strange, and undoubtedly only very temporary, twist of fate for the existing structure of holdings in the world to by itself come to match so closely the requirements of distributive justice – or for persons in the world to cooperate *voluntarily* to bring about that just distribution – that individuals were then in fact able to unilaterally ensure that others' rights to this just condition were not violated. In short, if we understand the moral duty of justice in this broader way, there is every reason to suppose that my discharging that duty (i.e., my not violating the rights of others to distributive justice) will require me to do my part in creating and supporting whatever national or international institutions might be available (or possible) to coercively bring about a just distributive condition for all (locally or globally). And there seems further to be good reason to suppose that my supporting the institutions that are necessary for doing justice in this way will require me to uniformly or regularly obey the rules by which those institutions promote justice. In short, discharging my duty to do justice implies a duty to obey the laws of justice-promoting institutions, including those of my home country.

The duty to obey begins to look like a natural consequence of a duty of justice, then, if we think of persons' moral rights not only as claims against others that those others not *personally* harm their interests, but also as claims against others that they help to ensure that all receive justice. On this conception, I do others an injustice – I wrong them or violate their rights – when I resist or fail to contribute to the establishment of a general institutional enforcement of rights. Here we approach the position defended by Kant and more recently by contemporary Kantians like Rawls.[33] As we

---

33 In addition to those theorists discussed later, Allen Buchanan has recently defended a similar view. Buchanan, reasoning from a general Kantian principle that all are entitled to equal respect and concern, defends a natural duty of justice that he understands as "a limited moral obligation to help ensure that all persons have access to institutions that protect their basic rights" (*Justice, Legitimacy, and Self-Determination*, 27, 86–92). Buchanan seems (unlike Kant and Rawls) to deny the possibility and the importance of deriving from this

have seen, other persons have a right, according to Kant, that we abandon the state of nature and do our part in creating and supporting an institutional structure that will legally (i.e., coercively) enforce our rights – that is, that will make real justice possible. While Kant was less concerned about distributive matters (such as equalizing material holdings) than are contemporary Kantians,[34] Kant was emphatically opposed to the (Lockean) idea that our duties can be discharged without our belonging to – and without our obeying the laws of – some civil (political) society. Others have rights that we quit our natural condition (in which we are a constant threat to them), that we help create and scrupulously obey the rules of the coercive legal system that alone can guarantee or "realize" their rights, and that we do nothing to weaken or undermine these essential institutions.

The Rawlsian Natural Duty of Justice

John Rawls offers a somewhat different (and mercifully less metaphysical) justification for his natural duty of justice than did Kant.[35] But he plainly agrees with Kant that we should understand our natural duties to require of us that we support and obey the rules of the coercive institutional structure that is necessary for justice to be done. There is no hint in Rawls that we could discharge the relevant duty of justice unilaterally in a state of nature (or in any other condition apart from membership in a political society). Indeed, where Kant worries prominently about the moral condition of persons in a state of nature, Rawls barely mentions the state of nature, except in noting the analogy between that idea's role in traditional social contract theory and the role of the "original position" in his own hypothetical contractarian theory of

natural duty any general moral duty to obey the law (238–40). But it is clear that he *means* only that there is no duty to obey owed to *government*. Buchanan argues that in a democracy (a form of government that is required as a matter of justice [256]), citizens have obligations owed to *each other* "to take compliance with the laws seriously" (253).

34 *Political Writings*, 75–6.
35 The arguments of this section draw on and extend those of Chapter VI of my *Moral Principles and Political Obligations*.

justice.[36] The moral duty of justice is "natural" for Rawls primarily in the sense that it binds persons regardless of their voluntary acts and that it holds between persons conceived of as moral equals (i.e., independent of "their institutional relationships").[37] Rawls begins his political philosophy with the (realistic) idea of persons already existing in a multiplicity of independent, territorial political societies, and he asks what can reasonably be required of persons (and, in his later work, of societies or "peoples") in such a condition. The duties of persons in their "natural condition" is simply not a central concern for Rawls.[38]

The "most important" natural duty under which each of us stands (in our current condition) is, according to Rawls, the natural duty "to support and to further just institutions." That duty requires the following:

> First, we are to comply with and to do our share in just institutions when they exist and apply to us; and second, we are to assist in the establishment of just arrangements when they do not exist, at least when this can be done with little cost to ourselves. It follows that if the basic structure of society is just,

36 John Rawls, *A Theory of Justice* (Cambridge, MA: Harvard University Press, 1971), 12.

37 Ibid., 114–15.

38 Since Rawls' theory of the "principles for individuals" (that is, of the duties and obligations that bind individual subjects) is in fact only a theory of the principles that would bind people in just political societies, that theory seems to directly imply nothing at all about the natural moral duties of persons living in seriously unjust societies or outside of political society altogether. And the natural duties actually discussed by Rawls are not "natural" in any very strong sense, but are only the "postinstitutional" moral duties that original position reasoners would select to bind themselves in their subsequent interactions. As such, much of the discussion to follow may seem to be aimed at a Rawls who is more Kantian than Rawls actually wished to be. But on my understanding of Rawls, there is no reason to accept the original position reasoning as yielding a morally interesting theory of justice (and of postinstitutional natural duties) unless persons have certain natural duties (and correlative natural rights) in the stronger sense discussed here. For instance, they must at least have the *pre*institutional duty to treat others as equals (or to deal fairly with them), or the original position construction will seem to have simply been drawn from (morally) thin air. I thus take Rawls to be committed to the existence of a preinstitutional, Kantian-style natural duty of justice (fairness, equal treatment), and my criticisms proceed accordingly.

or as just as it is reasonable to expect in the circumstances, everyone has a natural duty to do what is required of him. Each is bound irrespective of his voluntary acts, performative or otherwise.[39]

I will not try to elaborate here on what constitutes "the basic structure of society" for Rawls (Rawls may not have been entirely consistent in his various accounts of this idea) or on what would make such a structure "as just as it is reasonable to expect in the circumstances." Nor will I concern myself here with the obvious asymmetry between the second part of the duty, which is qualified with a cost limit (requiring action only if it costs us "little"), and the unqualified character of the first part of the duty (which appears to require compliance and doing our share, regardless of what this costs us).[40] We can, I suppose, assume for the moment with Rawls that compliance and doing our share will not, at least in reasonably just states, involve severe costs for individuals. Or we can suppose instead that the Rawlsian natural duty simply runs out once we have completed our routine, low-cost compliance (and so on), no longer binding us in the case of institutional demands for significant sacrifices.

It is sufficient for our purposes at this point to note that the natural duty of justice, as it was understood by Rawls, plainly does not imply an unqualified duty to obey the law ("to comply," to "do what is required") except in social conditions that come reasonably close to satisfying Rawls' famous two principles of justice.[41] In less just circumstances (which we might expect

---

39 Ibid., 334.
40 The asymmetry between the two parts of Rawls' natural duty of justice and the possibly high costs of legal compliance (when one considers laws like those requiring military service) both play central roles in George Klosko's attack on Rawls' Natural Duty account of political obligation (in "Political Obligation and the Natural Duties of Justice," *Philosophy & Public Affairs* 23:3 [Summer 1994]).
41 It might seem that we should question Rawls' insistence that the duty to comply binds us only in the case of reasonably just or near-just states. After all, considerably less just states may still do much of the same essential job that just states do in providing security, producing public goods, etc. After all, even the Third Reich enforced laws prohibiting murder, assault, and rape, provided some forms of poor relief, regulated commerce and traffic, etc. I suspect that

to characterize quite a number of existing societies), the natural duty of justice requires not obedience to law, but rather whatever low-cost assistance we can manage in helping to bring into existence reasonably just institutional structures. While assisting in this way might sometimes involve obeying the law, it might well require disobedience instead; the empirical circumstances and the requirements for effective assistance (dictated by those circumstances) would determine the specific actions required by the duty of justice. In any event, the duty of justice would imply no uniform duty to obey domestic law. Indeed, even in reasonably just societies, strict obedience to law may not be required by Rawls' natural duty, perhaps contrary to initial appearances. Rawls allows that while in near-just states the duty generally requires obedience even to particular unjust laws, obedience may not be required where the law's injustice is severely burdensome or where legal injustices fall disproportionately on one group of people (e.g., on permanent minorities).[42]

Let us focus for a moment on the second requirement of Rawls' duty of justice. Presumably, given that the duty applies to us independent of our "institutional relationships," the second part of the natural duty of justice requires that we assist in establishing just

Rawls' response would be the plausible contention that the second part of the duty will suffice to do any required work here – that is, the second part of the duty (requiring us to assist in establishing just institutions where they don't exist) will require us to comply with law even in unjust states, but only where doing so assists in making unjust institutions more just. Obeying the laws forbidding murder and rape might plausibly be expected regularly to do this (since murder and rape seldom advance the cause of justice, and since at least often anarchy must be avoided if we are to have any reasonable prospects of bringing into existence just institutions). But more general compliance in an unjust state would seem likely only to cause any movement toward justice to stagnate, so that a duty to promote justice could not include the kind of requirement of relatively strict compliance with unjust institutions that the first part of Rawls' duty specifies in the case of reasonably just ones. Interestingly, Kant apparently disagreed with Rawls on this, advocating as he did strict compliance even with the laws of tyrannical governments (*Political Writings*, 74–5, 83–7, 143–4).

42 Rawls, *A Theory of Justice*, 355. I will not discuss further the details of Rawls' account of the justifications for civil disobedience or conscientious refusal (see ibid., 350–91).

institutions not only for our own society, but for other societies as well.[43] While it may often be easier or more efficient to help in this effort close to home, the duty binds us to all persons (in their distinct societies) as moral equals. In this respect, then, the duty of justice has a structure similar to our normal understanding of moral duties of charity (or "mutual assistance"), where the needs of persons at a distance still fall fully within the scope of needs to which the duty requires us to attend.[44] Charity may begin at home, but it does not end there. It is possible, then, that the task of assisting in the establishment of just institutions may require us to devote our efforts to the needs of societies distinct from our own, especially where our own institutions are more nearly just than theirs (so that ours need less of our assistance than theirs in the push toward justice). And it seems possible as well that assisting other societies in this task might sometimes require of many of us actions that in fact involve disobedience to domestic law (for instance, where domestic law forbids private citizens to travel to or to interact in various ways with certain other nations, nations that might need significant assistance in establishing just institutions). This possibility would appear to bring the demands of the first part of the natural duty, which requires compliance with domestic law in near-just societies, into possible conflict with those of the second part.

How such a possible conflict between the two parts of the natural duty of justice is to be resolved Rawls does not appear to say.[45] Perhaps a legal system counts as unjust if it includes rules

---

43 Allen Buchanan apparently disagrees, taking Rawls' version of the natural duty to be less "robust" than his own (in part) because Rawls' duty requires support only for institutions that *apply* to one (Buchanan, *Justice, Legitimacy, and Self-Determination*, 87). As far as I can see, however, only the first part of Rawls' duty is ever qualified by him in this way.

44 In his diagram of "a full conception of right" (*A Theory of Justice*, 109), Rawls lists together in the category of "positive natural duties" the duties to "uphold justice," provide "mutual aid," and show "mutual respect."

45 Rawls' only apparent consideration of a conflict generated by the natural duty of justice concerns what he calls the conflict between "the duty to comply with laws enacted by a legislative majority" and "the right to defend one's liberties and the duty to oppose injustice" (ibid., 363). This sounds as if it should cover

that forbid morally mandated assistance to unjust or less just societies (though it is difficult, for me at least, to see why such laws
could not perfectly well flow from a domestic basic structure that
would count for Rawls as reasonably just). Perhaps we are to
assume that such laws would necessarily count for Rawls as imposing severe burdens of injustice on those compelled to refrain
from assisting other unjust or less just societies. But that suggestion, too, seems not at all plausible, leaving the Rawlsian position
on such conflicts obscure. On its face, then, the natural duty of
justice (as described by Rawls) seems vulnerable to charges of
internal inconsistency.

And there is a further tension between the two parts of this
Rawlsian natural duty. The first part of the duty requires of us
a particular set of acts, namely, those acts (and forbearances) required by our reasonably just domestic legal systems (along with
whatever acts constitute our share of supporting just domestic
legal and political institutions). But the second part of the natural duty of justice – the part requiring that we assist in creating just institutional structures – is most naturally read not as
requiring particular acts, but as setting an end to promote (or
specifying a moral property the occurrence of which to maximize).[46] Assisting in the establishment of just institutions would
then be understood simply as promoting the good of justice in the
world, either by trying to maximize the amount of justice in the
world or by keeping the ideal of a just world in mind in acting,
so that one regularly acts to advance that ideal. Promoting justice in these ways, of course, might or might not require uniform

the case I have in mind (where the duty to assist in promoting justice requires
us to violate domestic law). But the kind of justification for disobedience that
Rawls has in mind – roughly, that disobedience can sometimes actually help
to promote justice, as justice is understood by the very majority that made
the unjust law – seems inapplicable to the conflict between the duty to obey
domestic law and the duty to promote foreign justice.

46 Suggesting either a teleological/consequentialist duty – i.e., to maximize the
amount of justice in the world – or an imperfect deontological duty, with the
end of justice for all being the ideal to be kept in view in our choice of actions.
Given the Kantian character of Rawls' theory, the latter interpretation is, of
course, the more natural one.

performance of right-respecting acts – since it is at least possible that justice might sometimes be best promoted by performing unjust acts (such as harming those who are likely to innocently impede progress toward a more just state).

Now promoting or doing justice in this sense certainly might at first seem to require that we uniformly or regularly obey our countries' laws, for it is certainly possible that doing so is the best way to advance the cause of justice (where justice is understood as an obligatory end). So one might suppose that the first part of the duty – the duty of domestic compliance – could actually just be derived from the second part. Exactly what a duty to promote justice would require, though, seems to involve at least reasonably sophisticated empirical judgments about the likely consequences of various courses of action for the advancement of justice in the world. And it seems highly improbable that our conclusions would be the same for all citizens of all reasonably just states, given their very different capacities and circumstances. If that is true, however, it is hard to see how a *general* moral duty to obey the law – that is, a duty binding all or most persons in reasonably just political societies – could be plausibly derived from a natural duty to promote the end of justice. Making this even harder to understand is the simple fact that *local* obedience to law is not at all obviously even normally the best way for persons to promote the *global* end of justice.

Thinking of the second part of the duty as a duty to promote justice in this way suggests that the problems facing the Rawlsian derivation of a duty to obey the law from the natural duty of justice are even more general than my arguments thus far have suggested. For it is not at all clear why there should *be* two parts of a properly characterized natural duty of justice, two parts to come into possible conflict or stand in tension in the ways outlined previously. We can understand the motivating idea for the duty easily enough. Justice is an important moral good, "the first virtue of social institutions," to use Rawls' phrase.[47] A coercive institutional structure committed to securing persons' moral rights – or

---

47 Rawls, *A Theory of Justice*, 3.

multiple such structures in multiple autonomous political societies – is morally imperative; all persons, in consequence, have a duty to help bring about and uphold just institutions. But why then should those institutions that "apply to us" have some special moral claim on our attention? Justice is equally important everywhere. Why should we be thought to be specially bound to obey (and "do our share in") the domestic institutions that apply to us, as the first part of Rawls' duty asserts? What exactly privileges domestic institutions in this way? We can promote the cause of justice, advance the goal of a stable structure of just coercive institutions for all persons, without giving priority to the demands of domestic law. Perhaps promoting justice will regularly require conformity with domestic law, but perhaps it will not. Why is our natural duty not simply the general duty to advance the cause of justice as effectively as we can, by whatever means are most effective (at least where these effective means do not involve imposing on ourselves unreasonable costs)?

It appears, then, that in his formulation of the natural duty of justice Rawls is *presuming* the very duty to obey domestic law that is supposed to be *derived from* (or implied by) that logically prior duty of justice. There are, of course, many ways in which institutions can be said to apply to us. They can apply to us in the very minimal sense of merely naming us as falling within their scope or jurisdiction, as the NAACP might be said to apply to all persons of color. Or institutions could apply to us more strongly by both naming us and being accepted by us as applying to us, as is arguably true of most of our national legal and political institutions (at least in stable, affluent societies). Perhaps such acceptance is sufficient to give such institutions moral authority over us, so that we are obligated to act as they require us to act and to otherwise do our share in supporting them – though in my view this is true only if the acceptance in question amounts to a morally significant personal consent. But Rawls cannot be trying to ground in this way our duty to comply with just institutions that apply to us in our acceptance or consent. That would be to derive the duty to obey not from a natural duty, which requires no voluntary act (like acceptance or consent) to bind us, but rather

NATURAL DUTIES AND THE DUTY TO OBEY THE LAW   163

from a straightforwardly voluntaristic principle of *obligation* (such as Rawls' principles of fairness and fidelity[48]). And we know that Rawls in fact *rejects* claims that a general obligation to obey the law can be derived from principles of obligation,[49] quite apart from the fact that an implicit appeal to a voluntaristic principle of obligation would undermine Rawls' attempt to derive our duty to obey the law entirely from our natural duties.

For Rawls' argument to succeed, he must be able to identify something about the existence and application to us of our just domestic institutions that gives them privileged moral authority over us *without* (explicitly or implicitly) appealing to the special ways in which we might accept, consent to, or benefit from our domestic just institutions. And on the face of things, at least, it is hard to see what that something might be. It is certainly true that (by and large) American laws apply to Americans and French laws apply to the French. After all, American and French lawmakers specify or intend that (most of) their laws should be enforced only against their own citizens (qualified to cover resident aliens, visitors, diplomats, and so on). But it surely cannot be true that this legislative specification or intent is what grounds the relevant moral duties of obedience. For nobody, I assume, would seriously argue that if American lawmakers did in fact specify or intend that French citizens (in France) should pay American taxes, abide by American federal law, and so on, that the French would thereby have the same moral duty to obey as do resident American citizens.

There is no doubt, as Rawls contends, a profound difference "between those institutions . . . which must inevitably apply to us since we are born into them and they regulate the full scope of our activity, and those that apply to us because we have freely done certain things as a rational way of advancing our ends."[50] But why is the difference not that the latter institutions, unlike the former, have a *special* claim on our obedience and support

48 See again Rawls' diagram of his conception of right (ibid., 109).
49 Ibid., 113–16.
50 Ibid., 343–4.

(based in the voluntary acts by which we specially commit ourselves to them over other, possibly equally worthy, institutions)? Institutions to which we are simply *subject* by birth have only the coincidence of proximity to claim for themselves (beyond the brute, and I will suppose for now morally irrelevant, claim to superior power, to a superior ability to coerce and control – which advantage, it is worth remembering, domestic institutions need not always even possess). Why are the needs of domestic institutions for compliance, support, and assistance not on a moral par with the similar needs of foreign institutions, so that it is our effectiveness in advancing the cause of justice, not the proximity of our object institutions, that determines the nature of their moral claims on us (just as, I suppose, it is our ability to alleviate need and suffering, not the proximity of the needy, that determines what is required of us by our natural duty of charity or mutual assistance)? In short, why should there be a first part – a part that details our special moral relationship with domestic just institutions – of Rawls' natural duty of justice at all?

It is clear that in the first part of the natural duty of justice Rawls has in mind some *territorial* notion of application. Institutional rules generally have some explicit or implicit territorial limits of application. Indeed, many institutional rules really only make sense when understood in territorial terms (e.g., speeding laws prohibit speeding only on certain roadways; speeding in Europe does not violate American speeding laws). But to simply *assume* that anyone is bound to obey who is merely in the territory intended to be covered by a just institutional rule seems to simply beg the relevant questions: namely, why is legislative intent thought to be morally authoritative, or why are states' claims to territory sufficient to bind to obedience those who happen to be within the claimed territory? Most important, it is not at all clear how an institution's being *just* (or reasonably so) helps us to see who exactly is bound by its rules without appealing as well (and illicitly, for the purposes of Rawls' argument) to *other* morally interesting facts about people (their acceptance or consent, the institutional benefits they've enjoyed, etc.), facts that seem to provide *independent* grounds for asserting a duty to comply.

Of course, if our own legal and political institutions are just (or can be made just), and if we have a duty to promote justice, then it seems that we ought to support and assist our own just institutions as one way of promoting justice more generally. Indeed, as noted earlier, supporting our own institutions may well regularly be the most efficient way to promote justice, being less costly and less difficult to do so at home than abroad (though, we should add, it is not at all clear that we fail to discharge our natural duties simply by failing to adopt the most efficient means to accomplish the required moral task[51]). We can imagine, for instance, a world of multiple near-just political societies "dividing up" the universal duty to promote justice, with each country's population attending specially to its own just institutions – not because their own institutions are specially entitled to such attention, but simply because justice will be most effectively promoted by such an arrangement.[52] But notice that this happy picture assumes that populations in other countries will in fact do their duty and that their doing their duty will advance in equal measures their own institutions' march toward justice. What if others do not do their duty? Or what if, even after their populations do their best, some institutional structures simply need more assistance in becoming and remaining just than do others? The natural duty to promote justice would seem then – or, rather, now, since this is in fact the condition of the real world – to require not morally myopic continuing support exclusively for our domestic institutions, but rather that our low-cost assistance in the promotion of justice be carefully budgeted and targeted so as to be most effective in promoting justice. And that would seem likely to at least often involve directing our attention, support, and assistance not to our own happy near-just institutions, but to less happy societies.

51 I do not fail to discharge my natural duty to refrain from lying if I (inefficiently) refrain from communication with others altogether; and if I have a duty to keep my fair share of the world's needy at some modest level of well-being, I do not fail in my duty by using unnecessarily costly ways of helping (provided that I aid the right number of persons in the right measure).

52 So the assigned duties would be viewed "merely as an administrative device for discharging our general duties more efficiently" (Robert Goodin, "What Is So Special About Our Fellow Countrymen?", *Ethics* 98 [1988], 685).

Particularity and the Effects of Noncompliance

The problem for Natural Duty accounts (of the duty to obey the law) to which I point here is (part of) what I have elsewhere called the "particularity problem":[53] A general moral duty to promote justice – or any other impartial value – cannot bind one specially to support or comply with one particular state or society (such as "my own").[54] And the moral duty to obey the law is precisely such a particularized moral bond. This makes the derivation of a duty to obey domestic law from any natural duty desperately problematic from the start. Natural duties, remember, bind those who have them not because of anything those persons have done, or because of the special positions those persons occupy, but because of the moral character of the required acts. Happiness (utility) must be promoted because happiness is good. Murder must be refrained from because of the moral significance of murder. This means that natural moral duties will bind me as strongly with respect to persons or institutions that are not close to me (or my own) as they will with respect to those that are. Murdering Russians is as wrong as murdering Americans. Just Swedish political institutions merit support as much as, and for the same reason as do, just political institutions in the United Kingdom. But because this is true, it is difficult to see how a natural duty could ever bind citizens specially to their own particular laws or domestic institutions. It is easy to see why Socrates should promote justice. It is much harder to see why Socrates should specially support Athens or regard himself as specially bound by Athenian law if it really is after all the importance of *justice* that explains his duty.

Laws or governments or states being *ours*, of course, routinely have consequences that might well seem to explain our special

---

53 *Moral Principles and Political Obligations*, 31–5, 155–6.

54 This, of course, is precisely the point of Godwin's famous insistence that "that life ought to be preferred which will be the most conducive to the general good." In saving Fenelon rather than yourself, your brother, or your father, you save what is "more valuable" in terms of the impartial good at issue (in this case, utility). "What magic is there in the pronoun 'my', that should justify us in overturning the decisions of impartial truth?" (Godwin, *Enquiry Concerning Political Justice*, 169–70 [II.ii.]).

moral bonds to them. We may benefit specially from them, occupy roles in them, be relied upon specially by them in ways that are not true of other laws or governments or states. But these kinds of consequences all transparently involve appeal to transactional or associative facts about citizens and their domestic institutions, an appeal that a Natural Duty theory of the duty to obey cannot legitimately make. A natural moral duty might, of course, give us a quite contingent moral reason to specially obey and do our part in our domestic legal-political scheme if our own scheme happened to be the only scheme we could support while success-fully advancing the relevant impartial values; but this would not only make our particularized moral bonds depend on wild coinci-dences, it would make those bonds vary in strength and direction as international political and legal affairs changed. It would surely barely count at all as having explained our special moral duty to obey domestic law if we had to rely in our account on facts so contingent and changeable.

But perhaps we can explain our duty to obey domestic law *without* assuming that this moral duty has to be somehow spe-cial or exclusive. We would, admittedly, then have to give up our association of the duty to obey with ideas like patriotism, alle-giance, and loyalty. But why could we not just view our moral duty to obey domestic law as a nonprivileged part of the require-ment of a more general moral duty to promote some impartial value? After all, one can consistently satisfy the legal demands of more than one state at once, as holders of multiple citizen-ship routinely do. One can pay required taxes to more than one state, obey the laws of more than one state, even serve in the military of more than one state, and so on. What we cannot do, however, is to satisfy all of the *possible* reasonable legal re-quirements that might be imposed by more than one state si-multaneously, or discharge our basic legal duties where these are simply more restrictive than we might like them to be. No natural duty could consistently bind us to "serve (in the mili-tary, on a jury) when called" in more than one state. We can-not honestly accept an obligation to defend more than one state "against all enemies, foreign or domestic." Nor can we both obey legal commands from our government to refrain from dealing with, say, Iraq, and still satisfy the legal demands made by Iraq. It is in fact only political accommodation (or extraordinarily good fortune) that allows holders of dual citizenship to satisfy all of the legal demands of multiple states. We must understand the duty to obey the law as a special or particularized duty, and Natural Duty theories seem unable to generate a duty to obey so understood.

That, then, is the particularity problem faced by all Natural Duty theories of the duty to obey the law. But we should notice, further, that even if particularity were *not* a problem, a natural duty to promote justice or to support just institutions at home *still* would not appear to yield anything much like a uniform duty to obey the law even in a reasonably just society. For just institutions may sometimes be supported equally well or better by *non*compliance than by compliance. Rawls recognizes this in the case of unjust laws within basically just institutional structures, where disobedience may sometimes help to make near-just institutions more just. This is an important aspect of the Rawlsian justification for certain kinds of civil disobedience. But I would prefer to emphasize in this context the vastly more numerous and perfectly commonplace cases in which obedience or disobedience of domestic law is simply not likely to have *any* interesting effect, good or ill, on the stability, efficiency, or justice of a near-just institutional structure.[55] Typically, I think, it simply makes no difference to the cause of justice whether we obey or disobey the law. While legal disobedience may sometimes violate others' rights – and so constitute a breach of our narrower duty not to personally wrong others – even in those cases our disobedience seems routinely no more likely to affect the movement toward justice of our political and legal institutions than would obedience. Our individual actions simply have no appreciable effect at all on such matters. To be sure, were most people to similarly disobey, our institutions' ability to do justice would be impaired. But whether or not our duty to promote justice implies a duty for us to obey domestic law is presumably not a question whose answer

55 See Soper, *The Ethics of Deference*, 164.

turns on hypothetical conduct by others (particularly when that conduct is as unlikely as general legal disobedience).[56] Insofar as the duty is a duty to actually promote some end, whether or not it requires legal obedience must turn rather on the likely actual effects of our actions. And the actual effects of these actions, in typical contexts of general obedience, are normally negligible. One more act of legal disobedience or obedience simply makes no difference. Were I sufficiently influential that my obedient or disobedient actions were likely to be widely imitated, that might affect the argument. But I regret to report that I am not influential in that way. Nor, I suspect, are you.

The near-just (or, at least, the most just) legal and political structures with which most of us are familiar tolerate extraordinary amounts of noncompliance without obvious ill effects. Nor would small increments of increased obedience have obvious beneficial effects on those structures. Individuals can, of course, sometimes help to make their institutional structures better: perhaps by political activism of various sorts, by public support for those features of them that most make them just, by public protest of their flaws, and so on. And individuals can surely also help to undermine them, to slow institutional progress toward justice: say, by working to corrupt institutional officials, by organizing rebellion or widespread unjust disobedience, by publicly supporting their worst features, and so on. But normally, individual acts of legal compliance or noncompliance simply have no interesting role in this process at all. A single person's obedience of law would typically not make the system any better than would her disobedience. It is in the end unclear, then, just how the argument from a natural duty of justice to a duty to obey the law is supposed to proceed. Not only does a duty of justice seem ill equipped to tie us specially to our own local legal and political institutions in the required way. It also appears to be the wrong kind of duty to naturally yield a duty of simple legal compliance at all. In short, while there may well be a natural duty of justice, and one that

---

56 Here the same points are relevant that were raised earlier in our discussion of consequentialist generalization (in the section "Consequentialism").

can command a reasonable share of our moral attention, it seems not to be the place to look for the ground of our duty to obey domestic law.

Particularity and Salience

Jeremy Waldron has in a recent paper[57] attempted to defend Natural Duty theories of the duty to obey against just the kinds of criticisms I have made thus far, as has Christopher Wellman (in some of his papers[58] and, more directly, in the first portion of this book). Their accounts will be the subjects of the current section and the next, respectively. Waldron specifically mentions two objections to Natural Duty accounts of the duty to obey (and, more specifically, to Rawls' account) that he intends to answer: what he calls "the 'special allegiance' objection" and "the 'application' objection" (273–5). The special allegiance objection appears to be just what I have been calling the particularity problem that faces Natural Duty theories. The application objection is also one that is made earlier in my discussion of Rawls. If the attempted answer to the particularity problem is that only my own country's legal and political institutions apply to me (and that this application is what particularizes my duties to my own country), the move fails: There is no notion of application to appeal to in the answer that is not either straightforwardly question-begging or implicitly transactional (or associative[59]) in nature. Either way, a genuine and successful Natural Duty theory of the duty to obey the law cannot be completed.

---

57 "Special Ties and Natural Duties," in Edmundson (ed.), *The Duty to Obey the Law*. Page references for the paper in this section are given in parentheses in the text.

58 See especially "Liberalism, Political Legitimacy, and Samaritanism," *Philosophy & Public Affairs* 25:3 (Summer 1996), and "Toward a Liberal Theory of Political Obligation," *Ethics* 111:4 (July 2001).

59 Waldron does not in fact mention Associative accounts, instead dividing "philosophical accounts of what we owe the state" into just "two classes: theories of acquired obligation [by which he appears to mean Transactional theories] and theories of natural duty" (Waldron, "Special Ties and Natural Duties," 217).

Waldron begins his response to these objections by reminding us that we need to accept the idea of a natural duty of justice (of a Kantian–Rawlsian sort[60]) in order to make sense of certain firm intuitions about what we owe not just to our own countries, but to countries abroad. Most of us would agree that we have a moral duty to obey the laws of other countries when we are in them, as well as a duty not to undermine the just institutions of other countries (regardless of where we are). While a Transactional account can easily explain the first of these duties (in terms of the consent given on entering another country, say), only a natural duty of justice can explain the second. So we're obliged, if we take these intuitions seriously, to accept a natural duty not to undermine just institutions anywhere, including, of course, those in our own countries (275–8).[61]

Supposing we accept such a duty, however, how are we to defend it (as yielding a duty to obey domestic law) in the face of the two objections to such accounts? Waldron contends that some moral principles are "range-limited" rather than universally applicable, just as the legal principles of each particular country are normally limited in application to persons within that country's territories. We obviously need to justify such range limitation, since most moral principles apply to all persons equally. Waldron's justification appeals to Kant's political philosophy (some of the rudiments of which were summarized earlier). People who live side by side without just political and legal institutions over them

60 Waldron's version of the natural duty of justice appears to be weaker than (or is at least more explicit on the point than) Rawls' version in requiring that we support and comply with only those just institutions that are themselves required as a matter of justice (rather than binding us to every internally just institution that applies to us).

61 Strictly speaking, Waldron's claims here seem to me false. We could certainly explain the duty not to undermine the just institutions of other countries not in terms of a duty of *justice*, but simply in terms of a duty not to gratuitously harm others' interests – namely, the interests of those who live under and rely on the institutions. The justice of the institutions would not be required to explain the duty to refrain from sabotage (though the injustice of institutions might negate the duty or establish competing moral reasons for interference). However, I will not press this point here, since I in fact agree with Waldron that we have a natural duty not to undermine just institutions (anywhere).

are a constant threat to each other, even when they are trying to behave justly. So each person has a duty to establish and support just institutions in order to end this threat. But this duty is owed principally to those in one's immediate vicinity, since they are the ones directly threatened by one's conduct (280–1). Valid principles of justice, then, can be range-limited, imposing moral duties on those adjacent to one another that are not owed to everyone else.[62]

To administer such a range-limited principle of justice, we will need an institutional structure to deal with the claims of those grouped in some area, and this institution will have to enforce justice and resist attempts by others to compete with it in doing this task (282–3). The institution is entitled to the compliance and support of those with whose claims it deals if it is just, if it is capable of enforcing justice in the territory it claims, and if it is "legitimate" – by which Waldron appears to mean simply that there's good reason to recognize *it* as the one that should administer justice in the territory, that it is the *salient* solution to the problem of injustice. Such legitimacy/salience could be established by the institution's superior strength or by the popular support (actual or hypothetical) it commands (285–91). Each person thus has a (range-limited) natural duty of justice to support and comply with one *particular* just institution (or set of institutions) whose rules apply to him. The special allegiance (particularity) and application objections are answered, Waldron maintains. The correct answer to the question "Can an

---

62 I take Waldron's (or Kant's) argument here to be an attempt at an analogue of the more familiar argument that "impartialist" or "neutralist" moral theories (such as Kant's or utilitarianism) can in fact justify the familiar "special" obligations of friends, family members, neighbors, etc. in response to the charge that impartial moral principles cannot justify singling out some persons for special treatment. If the impartial value of friendship and love can justify special duties to those who are emotionally close to us, we might try to say, then the impartial value of justice can justify special duties to those who are physically nearby. The crucial difference between these cases, however, is that friendship and love (etc.) are *logically* tied to those close to us; injustice (and the undermining of or the failure to support just practices), by contrast, is equally a wrong to those physically near or far.

organization simply *impose* itself on us, morally, in this way?" is "yes" (292).

In considering Waldron's case, we would do well to note first just how many apparent problems he attempts to finesse with his notion of salience/legitimacy. Precisely who counts as being a special threat to someone else – a problem we might think extremely awkward for the account (am I a special threat to you, bringing me under Waldron's range-limited moral principle of special duty, if I live ten miles away from you? Or fifty miles? On the other side of a river or mountain? If I once hiked past your property or was told of your existence by a friend? Or only if I interact with you regularly?) – is an issue that is mysteriously converted in Waldron's account into the question of whose claims the salient just institution decides to deal with. This would appear to correspond to any morally interesting notion of what it is to be a threat to another only by the merest coincidence. Similarly, a state's (legal system's) legitimate territory would be determined according to which of the just institutions that claims that territory (and its residents) is most likely to enforce justice effectively there. And that appears to simply ignore all of the historical considerations (such as residents' actual consent, procedural conventions, etc.) that most of us take to be central to legitimate territorial sovereignty.

Worse, however, we need to remember that Waldron is attempting to rehabilitate a Natural Duty theory that purports to explain our moral duties to obey and support our *existing* legal and political institutions (at least where these are reasonably just). But there is simply no sense in which the territories or persons controlled by existing just institutions were ever sorted according to Waldron's categories – that is, according to who was most a threat to whom, or according to which territory would be most effectively governed by which institutions. The actual histories of all states' jurisdictional claims are instead replete with violence, injustice, and arbitrariness. Why, then, should we suppose that simply because certain institutions *now* are the salient enforcers of justice in a territory (having achieved and solidified that position by past acts of violent seizure and suppression of competition), such Kantian arguments (about threats and effective enforcement of justice) can justify special duties of obedience on all who are *currently* in that territory? We should suppose this, I think, only if we believe that historical facts are completely irrelevant to the legitimacy of present claims to authority and obedience. But most of us do not believe this. We believe that there is an enormous difference between the claims of an elected effective enforcer of justice and an equally effective (perhaps even equally popular) enforcer who takes power from an elected government by force. Such historical illegitimacy does not simply wear off over time. Further (as we saw earlier), actual governments have taken on many functions that have nothing obvious to do with the task of administering justice. So the scope of any authority they might wield, as this authority might be legitimated by Waldron's arguments, would appear to be far more limited than the authority actually claimed by modern states; and our duties to obey would seem to be correspondingly limited.

But suppose we set to one side such concerns about the history and nature of existing political and legal institutions, and about the lack of correspondence between their claims to obedience and the moral categories that justify such claims in the Kantian argument. Can Waldron's argument then justify (in Natural Duty terms) his claims of a special, particularized duty to obey? In my view, it cannot succeed even so qualified. Consider more carefully the central claim of the Kantian Natural Duty argument: that I wrong those around me (by threatening them with injustice) if I decline to authorize institutions to enforce justice among us (and thus refuse to undertake a moral duty to comply with such institutions).[63] First, of course, the idea that we are special threats to those who are near us – which is what allegedly particularizes (localizes) our general duties, binding us specially to domestic institutions – seems both inherently implausible and a bit dated. It is precisely with those near me that I am most likely

63 Notice that there is an apparent gap in the Kantian argument: namely, that between having a duty to authorize institutions of justice and having actually authorized such institutions. Presumably the Kantian will (must?) contend that those who are obligated to consent to X have a duty to act as their actual consent to X would obligate them to act.

to have established bonds of friendship or sociability, making me less of a threat to them than to others. And it is precisely with those near me that I am most likely to have frequent and ongoing interactions, making aggression against any of their number irrational, even should I have nothing but purely self-regarding motivations (that is, the rational strategy for individuals in the ongoing "Prisoner's Dilemma" of social life will usually be social cooperation – because that dilemma is iterated and without an obvious endpoint rather than being a "single-play" dilemma). Further, of course, I can as easily mail letter bombs or anthrax to someone in Asia as I can to those nearby. And surely other states or their evil (e.g., terrorist) residents constitute greater threats to us than do harmless local nonparticipators (arguing, perhaps, precisely *against* institutions establishing purely local sovereignty and control, just as do concerns about a just distribution of resources across the world's population).

Vastly more important (and more surprising, given the argument's distinguished history), however, is the more general implausibility of the claim that every person wrongfully threatens others (near or distant) wherever they live together without mutual commitment to institutions for enforcing justice. Being a threat to others in a way that wrongs them is an objective notion. We do not wrong others simply by virtue of their subjective *feeling* of being threatened by us (which is, perhaps, the source of the mistake). I can, conceptually, feel threatened by anything (say, by the robin on my lawn), provided only that it appears dangerous to me. But the dangerous-looking man who passes me in the dark alley surely does me no moral wrong simply because he is the object of my fear. He must actually be likely (in a special way) to harm me before he could possibly be accused of wronging me.

So how, exactly, do those who refuse to authorize institutions to settle their claims constitute wrongful threats to others? Even in a pure, apolitical state of nature, I think, it would often be true that particular persons (those, say, who were nonviolent, sociable, or squeamish) simply could *not* be said to be threats to others. That others might nonetheless feel threatened by them is as irrelevant to the Kantian argument as my fear in the dark alley is to ascriptions of wrongdoing there. (And, in any event, those others might certainly have good grounds for believing some persons not to be threats at all.) But we do not live in an apolitical state of nature. And it is even more implausible here and now to contend that each person who refuses to authorize legal institutions is a wrongful threat to others. Those who refuse such authorization will be held as fully accountable under domestic law as will those who cheerfully accept their duty to obey. They will be as fully deterred as anyone can be deterred by the threat of legal punishment and social sanctions. In denying the law's authority over me, I surely am no more of a threat to others than is someone who accepts that authority while frequently ignoring his acknowledged moral duties. More generally, the combination of a person's peaceable character and the law's deterrent effects would seem to completely discredit the charge that that person was an objective (wrongful) threat to others, simply by virtue of insisting on her natural freedom in the face of the claims of domestic legal and political institutions.

But what of the possibility of moral disagreement (which is much emphasized by Kantians)? Those who accept the authority of a "neutral" umpire – that is, the salient domestic institutions for enforcing justice – might rightly fear that one who declines to accept it, even when she is conscientiously trying to do justice, would harm them because of her different conception of justice. This concern seems to me dramatically overstated by Kantians (and not only because law and society deter equally those subject to and those free of the law's authority). First, of course, if her different conception of justice is the *correct* conception, she cannot possibly *wrong* me by successfully acting on it (however little I may like what she does). But suppose her conception is not correct. Still, the worry here is supposed to be about the threat posed by genuinely conscientious conduct, not by the conduct of scoundrels and self-serving rationalizers. And there is in fact reasonably broad agreement among competing conceptions of justice on at least its core requirements (concerning nonaggression toward innocents); so the injuries she does me while acting conscientiously (supposing she is not kept in line by legal threats) seem unlikely to be severe. But even were this not so, one who conscientiously strives to be just (according to a conception of justice different from my own) is both far more predictable than the unconscientious – and so far less of a threat to me – and far less of a hazard to me than are those who share my conception of justice, but act on it only sporadically, and those who are committed to no conception of justice at all. So the idea that one somehow becomes a *special* threat simply by denying the state's authority seems entirely indefensible.

But justice cannot be done, the Kantian will reply, without institutions to enforce people's rights. And the institutions that secure justice require support and compliance. This can all be granted (though I hope the text makes clear the ways in which I actually want to resist the former assertion[64]). But even granting this much, it is still insufficient to establish that particular individuals have a duty to comply with their local (reasonably just) legal and political institutions when these already exist and enjoy general compliance (or even to establish a duty to help create such institutions where others are successfully engaging in doing so). My (or your) not being subject to the state's authority, not having a duty to obey it, cannot "undo" the justice the state secures (or will secure). So, if he is not to simply beg the question we are

---

64 Justice, for Kant (and, presumably, for Kantians), consists in each person's having that to which she has a legitimate moral claim – physical security and "external freedom," the resources necessary for pursuing a reasonable, just life, etc. Justice cannot (despite Kant's occasional lapses) consist of the *institutional* provision of these goods without the definition's simply begging the question at issue between Lockeans and Kantians. The Kantian claim must be rather the empirical claim that institutional enforcement is the only way to genuinely secure people's legitimate claims. People are not entitled to any more than having their rights respected. They are not entitled to having them respected in a certain way (e.g., happily, institutionally). If security requires an institutional framework, it certainly does not require this *naturally* or *necessarily*, but only contingently, in typical social contexts involving persons with limited powers and resources (that is, it is certainly possible to *imagine* how one might be made secure in a state of nature). So obedience to or creation of just institutions cannot be part of the very content of a natural duty of justice. That is one of the problems with the formulations of the natural duty in, e.g., Rawls and Buchanan.

exploring, the Kantian Natural Duty theorist must maintain that simply in consequence of remaining free of duty and subjection to the state and the law, I wrong those around me. Kant (and Waldron) try to maintain this by the wrongful threat argument we have just considered and rejected.

Another broadly Kantian possibility, of course, is to argue that the wrong in question is not one of being a threat to those around me, but rather of riding free on their submission and sacrifice. I treat others unfairly when I decline to do my part in the moral project of justice by declining to undertake a duty to obey the law (support the government, etc.). Why should I be left free of duty while I enjoy equally the fruits of others' efforts to maintain the institutions that secure justice for all? This, as we will see, is the move made by Wellman (at a similar point in his "samaritan" Natural Duty theory), and I will respond to that charge of unfairness in the next section.[65] For now, however, it is sufficient to see that the Kant–Waldron version of the Natural Duty argument depends crucially on its "wrongful threat premise: Those who refuse to sign up, denying the authority of the salient justice-enforcing institutions, wrong those around them by being threats to them. It is this premise that supports the claim that our natural duties

---

65 Buchanan also seems (at one point) to try to deal with the particularity problem in this way. But he also offers a more limited and different kind of solution. In democracies, he argues, failure to comply with domestic law (without "weighty reasons" for noncompliance) shows "a disregard for our fellow citizens," citizens who, participating in a system that treats all as equals, authorized the making of that law (Buchanan, *Justice, Legitimacy, and Self-Determination*, 255). And where institutional resources do not allow for democracy, mere salience (of the sort Waldron has in mind) will suffice to particularize our natural duty of justice (258). But Buchanan gives no real reasons why salience should be thought to have this morally particularizing effect (or, rather, he gives none that have not already been countered in the preceding text). And your legal noncompliance, even in a democracy, shows "disregard" (disrespect) for your fellow citizens only if you are legitimately subject to the egalitarian institutional process for making law in which they participated. I show no disrespect to persons who democratically pass rules for conduct in their neighborhood if I am not part of their neighborhood – that is, unless they actually have the authority to make rules that bind me. And it is that prior question of local authority – the question Buchanan wants to set aside (237–40) – that is crucially implicated in concerns about particularity.

can be particularized to imply a moral duty of domestic legal compliance. But that crucial premise of the argument is false.

Obedience and Rescue

Perhaps, though, the Kantian Natural Duty theorist could emphasize less the threat of positive harm to others posed by those who deny a duty of obedience, emphasizing instead the kind of negative harm done to others by those who refuse to pull together. I can fail to show obligatory respect to others not only by threatening to positively aggress against them. I can also be disrespectful by ignoring their danger or suffering (indeed, it is hard to imagine how I could show less respect for another than by allowing her to perish when I could prevent it with little or no effort or cost). And where saving another from great and unmerited harm requires my participation in a collective effort, the failure to participate would seem to constitute such wrongful disrespect. Perhaps, finally, our domestic legal and political institutions (at least when they are reasonably just) are properly characterized as coordinating precisely this kind of collective effort to rescue others from great and unmerited harm, so that we are all morally bound to do our parts in creating and supporting such institutions. The Kantian respect relevant to this case is not respect for legal officials or the respect shown others by refraining from aggression against them. It is the respect we owe to those in peril. This appears to be (roughly) the view of my coauthor, Christopher Wellman. His Natural Duty case for a moral duty to obey domestic law appeals not to the natural duty of justice, but rather to another of the natural duties mentioned by Rawls: namely, the natural duty of mutual aid.

Wellman accepts the necessity of the state (and its legal and political institutions) for the supply of crucial goods – most importantly, security and the neutral umpire's guarantee "that all those in spatial proximity play by the same rules" (Chapter 2). Further, he argues, the costs of having a state imposed upon us are considerably less than the benefits gained by (virtually) all of us, as we can see if we imagine having to choose between accepting such subjection and having our state immediately dissolved. Thus, the coercion employed by the state to accomplish its ends is "both (1) necessary to save everyone in [the state's] territory from the perils of a lawless environment and (2) is not an unreasonable imposition upon those coerced." And since (the permissive part of) the principle of samaritanism establishes that we are morally permitted to rescue someone from serious peril where in doing so we do not unreasonably impose on others, the state (when reasonably just) employs its coercive powers permissibly. The state, as rescuer, enjoys legitimacy.[66]

Wellman rightly acknowledges, however, that this argument cannot yet supply us with an account of the duty to obey the law. (State legitimacy, understood in this way as just the moral permissibility of ruling, does not correlate with duties of others to comply with state rule.) So Wellman adds to the argument the further premises of (a) the moral duty of rescue (the requiring part of the samaritan principle) and (b) fairness in the distribution of the burdens of samaritanism. We have a natural moral duty to perform easy rescues of those in serious peril when we are well positioned to do so, Wellman maintains. Since it is only our collective obedience to law that can rescue our fellow citizens from the perils of a lawless state, we have a (collective) duty to obey the law, legal obedience being an easy (i.e., low-cost) response to their plight. While no particular individual's obedience is required to thus maintain the rule of law, still fairness requires that we each do our share of this "communal samaritan chore"; it is unfair that some enjoy "the good of discretion" while others do their parts and obey. Legal obedience is our fair share of the morally required task. This style of Natural Duty argument, Wellman believes, permits him to solve the particularity problem. Since the problem of lawlessness must be solved locally (i.e., by multiple territorial sovereigns), and since that solution is

---

66 Wellman seems not to favor the term "legitimate" in this essay, preferring to refer to the state's being morally justified in using or morally permitted to use coercion. But such moral permissibility is, of course, one (weak) notion of state legitimacy; and Wellman uses the language of legitimacy to make the same point in the papers cited in Footnote 58.

unavailable if all in a territory use their discretion in deciding how to act, each person has a duty particularized to local compliance.

Some of these claims, it should be clear, are vulnerable to the arguments I've advanced in previous sections. One point at which Wellman's account seems distinctively and immediately vulnerable, however, is in his contention that legal obedience constitutes an appropriately easy or low-cost sort of rescue of our fellow citizens (it being allowed all around, apparently, that risky or costly rescues are morally optional, not obligatory).[67] Wellman admits that states "sometimes make considerable demands" on their citizens (an apparent high cost), but he believes that the substantial benefits of citizenship, subtracted from these possibly costly demands, permit us to view "the *net* costs as not unreasonable" (Chapter 2). This seems to me an odd form for Wellman's argument to take, for several reasons. First, of course, Wellman has allowed that "unusual valuers" may in fact not stand to benefit at all (on balance) from the state's stability, so presumably they must be excused from contributing to the collective rescue efforts (which, I suppose, might not much trouble Wellman, since such valuers are, after all, unusual).

Second, though, and far more telling, there seems to be a serious problem with the fashion in which Wellman computes the costs of obedience in this argument. Strictly speaking, of course, according to Wellman's computation, the costs involved are not just low (not just "not unreasonable") but must actually be nonexistent. The benefits of citizenship (including the enormous good of security) minus the costs of obedience are, for Wellman, a very positive sum. But the oddness of claiming that legal obedience has *no* cost simply highlights the relevant mistake. In classifying possible acts of rescue as easy or costly, we are normally

---

67 George Klosko has also criticized Wellman for his handling of this cost limitation ("Samaritanism and Political Obligation: A Response to Christopher Wellman's 'Liberal Theory of Political Obligation," *Ethics* 113:4 [July 2003]); but Klosko's critique, I think, strikes Wellman's case at the wrong place (worrying about his including in the computation of costs the benefits to rescuers themselves) and in the wrong way (complaining that this move guts Wellman's antipaternalism).

identifying the prospective costs from the perspective of a typical passerby. We are trying to see when it is reasonable to expect a normally self-interested person to act exclusively in the interest of others. So calling the police, unlocking an exit from a burning building, dropping a rope from the pier to a drowning woman, and so on might normally qualify as involving low costs (or risks). Rescuing people from the top floor of a fiercely burning building would normally not so qualify (nor would we dream of morally condemning a passerby for failing to race to such a rescue).

But individual citizens, doing their parts in the collective task of maintaining the rule of law, never confront a choice between bearing the costs of obedience or bearing the costs of a lawless state of nature. Individual disobedience (failure to rescue) virtually never has as a likely cost the collapse of the state. Instead, the prospective costs of obedience must be calculated keeping the *actual* costs of disobedience in mind; and the actual costs of individual disobedience (as Wellman concedes) are normally negligible. The relevant calculation for an *individual*, then, will often show the costs of legal obedience to be (in Wellman's word) "considerable." Perhaps one might claim that the cost to the *collective* (i.e., the society) of *collective* disobedience would be high enough to make *collective* obedience an act with low costs. But it is not collective acts or collective duties (however we might try to understand these) whose costs we should be assessing. Our (i.e., Wellman's) question is whether or not *individuals* have a duty to obey. And if individuals' obedience is to be required of them by their natural duty to perform easy rescues (or, in this case, to do their share of easy rescues), we must calculate easiness in terms of individuals' actual likely costs. The cost of a Hobbesian state of nature is simply irrelevant to that calculation.

I believe that the reason it might be hard to see such points – or even to follow the arguments in which they are made – is that there is a much deeper problem with Wellman's case. Even leaving aside concerns about the costs of doing our duty, Wellman seems in the end to be employing a version of a duty of rescue (or mutual aid) that is quite idiosyncratic and morally suspect. The duty actually used in his arguments concerning a duty to obey the law is not the same as the moral commonplace to which

Wellman appeals in his examples; and, indeed, the specific form of Wellman's duty seems to be inspired primarily by his argumentative needs, not by independent reasons to believe such a duty exists.

As our general (i.e., noncontractual, nonreparative), positive moral duties to others are normally understood (by those who accept at all the existence of such duties), these duties are of two sorts. There are, in the first place, general duties of charity (mutual assistance) or beneficence. Second, there are duties of rescue (or, if you prefer, samaritan duties or duties of mutual aid). Duties of charity are duties to alleviate suffering or need. They are generally understood as imperfect duties, owed to no particular rightholder (since all equally needy persons seem to have equally strong claims on available resources), but owed rather to persons generally (or owed to nobody, but just morally imperative). For those who defend such duties, the chief problem has always been how to limit their apparent demands. There are far too many desperately needy persons in the world for me to help them all; but limiting my responsibility to the needy persons I actually encounter seems far too hard on residents of India and far too easy on residents of American gated communities. So duties of charity have generally been thought to be limited in either the specific resources on which they have a claim – we must only give our "surplus" resources, those beyond what we need for moderately comfortable lives (as Locke held) – or by the idea that we owe only a fair share of the overall task of eliminating dire need – if we have done our part (even if others do not do theirs), our duty to give to the needy is (at least for the moment) discharged. Governmental institutions (if they did not themselves tend to inefficiency) might be useful for coordination of this moral task (e.g., for efficiently collecting and distributing charitable contributions); but we can plainly all do our duties of charity without such institutions, given the many private charitable agencies and the (admittedly sometimes daunting) possibility of personal charitable activity.

Duties of rescue, by contrast, are generally understood to be moral duties to deal with emergencies (rather than with ongoing problems like poverty). Where others find themselves facing occasional serious harm, and where we can prevent this without great cost or risk, we are morally bound not to pass by. Indeed, those in peril may be thought to have a *right* to be rescued (i.e., the duty is often characterized as a perfect duty). But this right could not intelligibly be thought to be held against everyone. People separated from the emergency by lack of knowledge or by significant distance could not possibly be said to have breached some right of the imperiled, for they could do nothing to help. As a result, duties of rescue are normally said to bind us only in situations where we are specially positioned to accomplish an easy rescue (as in familiar face-to-face rescue cases). This implies, of course, that such duties cannot be thought to bind us to perform our fair share of required rescues. We cannot anticipate emergencies in a way that would permit the distribution of the relevant burdens. The moral burdens simply fall (perhaps quite unequally) on those who happen to be present at the emergencies (or have the knowledge that allows them to make themselves present). Notice that the very idea of institutions administering such a duty (by collection and distribution) makes no sense in this case. The most institutional rules can do is to enforce the duty (by punishing those who fail to assist the imperiled when they find themselves positioned to do so).

Wellman's samaritan duty seems to be a curious hybrid of these two kinds of positive duties. His examples are all of rescues, not of charity, suggesting (as the samaritan terminology implies) that he has in mind a duty of this second sort. And the face-to-face character of duties of rescue is plainly supposed to *localize* the moral duty in a way that will permit Wellman (in using this duty to explain our duty to obey the law) to deal with the particularity problem. But the actual content of the duty Wellman describes is more like the content of a duty of charity – that is, a fair share of a collective moral task. And the duty seems to be owed not to persons whose emergencies we actually confront, but to all persons in our political communities. Finally, the moral task to which Wellman thinks the duty is addressed is an ongoing problem (of providing security [and other public goods] for all), not the kind of local, occasional task to which duties of rescue seem to be addressed.

So Wellman's natural samaritan duty seems to be neither fish nor fowl. There is an obvious initial problem of motivating the assertion that such a duty actually exists, since it seems to lack the support of the commonsense moral intuitions that have led moral theorists to carefully distinguish the two kinds of positive duties. But worse, only if the duty is understood in one way – as a duty to address an impersonal, ongoing, nonoccasional moral problem – does it make sense to understand its content as a fair share of the overall task, while only if it is understood in a different way – as a duty to confront the emergencies actually directly presented to us – does it make sense to see the duty as localized and owed to our fellow citizens (rather than also to those abroad, who are equally in need of security, and so on). If the task in question is impersonally important, then it is important everywhere, and a contribution to it that I make anywhere, not just locally, is a good thing. If what matters is rather that I show special respect for those whose peril I actually confront (and can prevent), then fairness in the distribution of such a moral burden seems simply irrelevant. Further, of course, the emergency Wellman thinks we are duty-bound to prevent is not of the face-to-face sort; I actually confront or know about the situations of only a tiny percentage of my fellow citizens (my knowledge is, in fact, much more like the knowledge I have of ongoing material need in the world). And I can neither unilaterally prevent the relevant harm nor unilaterally permit it to occur. Lawlessness will neither result from nor be prevented by my individual conduct. In short, the emergency is not really properly described as an emergency at all.

Let me expand on these concerns by considering more carefully the use made by Wellman in his arguments of the ideas of fairness and fair shares.[68] It makes sense to speak of an individual owing a fair share of some task, in my view, only if that individual is morally bound to some group or collective entity and its

---

68 Buchanan, while rejecting the duty of rescue utilized by Wellman as too minimal a requirement (*Justice, Legitimacy,* and *Self-Determination*, 248n), appears to agree with Wellman in insisting that persons have a duty to bear their fair share of the collective local moral tasks (ibid., 92–3). Thus the arguments advanced here against Wellman's use of the idea of fairness seem to apply equally (*mutatis mutandis*) to Buchanan's position.

enterprises. Others cannot demand of me that I do my part unless I actually *have* a part in some scheme or enterprise to which
I am bound. When we speak of a person owing her fair share of
the charity needed to relieve suffering, for instance, this is intel-
ligible because we can think of all persons as naturally bound to
humanity (naturally bound to show respect to all others, say) and
think of the relief of suffering as a morally mandated task for that
collectivity. But consider now Wellman's insistence that persons
owe a fair share of the *local* task of saving local persons from the
evils of lawlessness. Such an appeal to fairness here can be plausible only if either (a) all persons are naturally bound to their *local*
political groups and the local tasks of those groups or (b) persons
have *special* obligations of fairness (or fair play) to do their parts
in their local political schemes. If (b) is true – that is, if our local
polities really qualify as genuinely cooperative schemes and we
as participants in them – then we can account for our duty to
obey by straightforward appeal to a fairness theory of obligation.
Not only would this make the account a member of the Transactional (reciprocation) family, not a Natural Duty account, we
know that Wellman thinks such accounts fatally flawed[69] (and
in this, as we have seen, I agree with him). That leaves possibility (a) to explain the role that fairness is playing in Wellman's
argument. But holding (a) simply involves *presuming* the particularity of the relevant natural duty, which is precisely the point
at issue. Wellman's argument is supposed to *conclude* with a particularized natural duty (and a consequent moral duty to obey).
The argument cannot legitimately utilize (part of) its conclusion
as an implicit and unargued premise.

So even if there were a genuine natural moral duty with the
curious hybrid character of Wellman's samaritan duty, it could not
be claimed to be a duty that bound persons to do their fair shares
of a communal task without either just begging the question at
issue or in the process supporting an alternative and radically different approach. We can, of course, try to preserve the Kantian
"feel" of Wellman's Natural Duty argument by insisting that just

---

69 Wellman, "Toward a Liberal Theory of Political Obligation," 737–8.

as doing justice is humankind's collective moral task, so is rescuing humankind from the perils of a lawless state of nature. Each
person must do her part in this collective task. But accepting that
much (as we have seen) simply does not imply that our parts must
have *local* obedience as their first and principal content. If we concentrate on humankind's ongoing need for security, Wellman has
identified too small a group (our fellow citizens) as owed any duty
aimed at that need. Those abroad share in that need, and I can
contribute in a variety of ways to alleviating it nonlocally. If we
concentrate instead on the morality of our face-to-face human
interactions, then Wellman has identified too large a group as
owed our moral attention. Only a few fellow citizens are directly
affected by my conduct.

In short, the particularity problem is still not addressed. Indeed, Wellman's problems would not be solved even if we conceded a moral duty of rescue with the kind of content imagined by
Wellman. Suppose that I *am* morally bound to do my fair share in
preventing the *local* emergency of lawlessness (i.e., suppose possibility [a]). How might I go about this? To Wellman the answer
is obvious: To prevent lawlessness, one obeys the law; obedience
is the *only* way to do our part, since political coercion is the *only*
solution to lawlessness. But the good my obedience is supposed to
provide to others, remember, is the good of security. And it is not
at all clear that such a good could not be provided for another by
means other than legal obedience. Since the number of persons
needing security is at worst three or four times greater than the
number duty-bound to help provide it, my fair share of helping
to provide security could be done by providing security for, say,
myself and two or three others. And surely I could accomplish
this in other ways than by obeying and thus providing a tiny
increment of the security experienced by all (when all obey the
law). Why could I not provide it more directly, by helping in more
substantial ways to protect from violence by others those individuals I interact with locally (or even, more fancifully, by building
a secure compound in which I invite some others to stay)? That
few might choose such means of satisfying their duty (over the
easier course of legal obedience) is irrelevant. What is relevant

is that a duty of rescue, even understood as Wellman understands it, cannot be said to directly imply a duty to obey the law.

Even more to the point, however, why can I not simply do the duty described by Wellman just by scrupulously refraining from violence (deception, etc.) toward others (and letting others see my intentions in this regard), while acknowledging no duty at all to *obey* the law? Since legal coercion and a sense of duty can assure my fellow citizens of my doing no more than this in any event, how can it be that my anarchist refusal to *obey* constitutes a failure to do my part in contributing to the security of all? We should not be seduced here by the Kantian argument into confusing means with ends. It is not legal *obedience* that is the moral goal in question, though the Kantian argument may sometimes be (question-beggingly) presented as if this is the case. Obedience is only a *means* to general enjoyment of the good of security. If one can do one's part in promoting that good *without* obeying the law, one has surely in so doing discharged any moral duty one might have. The facts (if they are facts) that states are necessary (to coerce the evil, the partial, and others who do not or cannot respect persons generally) and that states need a certain level of compliance to function effectively might *seem* to affect this conclusion. But they do not. Nor does the fact (if it is a fact) that everyone's using his discretion in genuinely trying to treat others well would cause chaos. What moral duty requires of us is a function of our actual circumstances. And if our actual circumstances permit us to effectively promote morally mandated ends (such as need satisfaction, security, or even local security) without adopting the usual (or locally prescribed) means of doing so, then we are plainly permitted to. Were our circumstances different – if, say, our state were in danger of collapse – then so might be the specific acts required by morality. As things stand, however, even were we to grant Wellman the kind of moral duty he describes, such a duty would not imply that typical persons in typical states are morally required to obey the law.

8   Conclusions

I have discussed the principal variants of Natural Duty theories of the duty to obey the law that are being defended by contemporary political and legal philosophers/theorists. But the influence of this family of theories in fact appears to extend well beyond the self-proclaimed family members. Many theories of the duty to obey that are presented by their defenders in Associative or Transactional language seem in actuality to rest more heavily on Natural Duty foundations. Let me note here just two prominent recent examples of this tendency. The best-known recent defense of an (allegedly) Associative account of the duty to obey – namely, Dworkin's – appears to justify its support for the moral force of Associative ties precisely by appealing (non-Associatively) to a "natural duty" that we have "to honor our responsibilities under social practices that define groups and attach special responsibilities to membership."[1] Similarly, George Klosko's prominent recent defense of a fairness theory of obligatory obedience[2] (which purports to be a Transactional reciprocation theory [to use my classifications]) seems actually to be far less concerned with fairness, properly understood, than with the needs of those who depend on the public goods states provide. It is the value or importance of these public goods (their "presumptive" status) – and some unacknowledged natural duty to

1 *Law's Empire*, 198.
2 *The Principle of Fairness and Political Obligation* (Lanham, MD: Rowman & Littlefield, 1992).

help make them generally available in our society – that seems to ground required obedience in Klosko's theory, not (as should be the case if fairness is really the issue) our acceptance of benefits, our free participation in a genuinely cooperative scheme, or the ways in which refusal to obey would take advantage of others.[3]

So the arguments presented here (against Natural Duty accounts of a duty of legal obedience) may reach more widely than is immediately evident. The conclusion to which those arguments point – when conjoined with those summarized previously against Associative and Transactional accounts – is that there is (for most persons in most states) no moral duty to obey the law. This is the position commonly referred to as philosophical anarchism.[4] Most nontheorists, I've suggested, are probably initially disinclined to accept such a conclusion, perhaps because they think it implies that legal disobedience is routinely or always morally justifiable. And in one technical sense this is correct: If "disobedience" means literally "not *obeying* the law" – that is, not doing what law commands because law commands it – then the denial of a duty to obey does in fact entail that disobedience (so

---

3 See my arguments to this effect in "Fair Play and Political Obligation: Twenty Years Later" (in *Justification and Legitimacy*) and *On the Edge of Anarchy*, 251–60. Klosko has recently argued that defenses of a duty to obey that rely on a moral duty of rescue (such as Wellman's) must inevitably accept the truth of premises that are sufficient to motivate Klosko's own fairness theory of the duty to obey ("Duties to Assist Others and Political Obligations," *Politics, Philosophy & Economics* 3:2 [2004–5]). So he proposes that rescue theories should function as a supplement to fairness theory, reversing the order of priority defended by Wellman. Klosko may be correct that rescue theories (like Wellman's) rest on the same premises as his own fairness theory. But that is only because, in my view, Klosko's theory is not really a *fairness* theory at all. It is in fact a disguised Natural Duty theory, resting on an unstated moral duty to help supply essential goods locally – and is thus indistinguishable in its foundational assumptions from theories like Wellman's. As such, Klosko's theory is vulnerable to the same arguments, presented earlier, that defeat other Natural Duty theories.

4 I explain and defend this view in my "Philosophical Anarchism," in *Justification and Legitimacy*. I in fact prefer to identify philosophical anarchism with a particular (weak) understanding of the denial of state legitimacy. But because state legitimacy, in its traditional sense, is the set of rights that (in part) correlates with subjects' duties of obedience, denying state legitimacy (with respect to most persons) entails the denial of most persons' duties to obey.

understand) is normally justified. But if by "legal disobedience" we mean simply "not performing the act (or forebearance) identified by the law as obligatory," then nothing so dramatic about the moral justification of disobedience to law in fact follows from my conclusion. For, as we have seen, we often have good moral reasons, and even moral duties or obligations, to perform in the ways the law makes institutionally obligatory.[5] We have good moral reasons not to harm or deceive innocent persons, to promote justice, feed the hungry, and rescue the imperiled, quite apart from the law's requirements and prohibitions, just as we have (weaker) reasons not to unreasonably offend, inconvenience, or frustrate others. A duty to obey the law would add only another kind of reason to those (normally sufficient) reasons we already have for respecting others and treating them well. The real "bite" of philosophical anarchism – the place where its denial of a duty to obey seems to require a real divergence from the practical recommendations of those who defend such a duty – is in the cases of distinctively political legal requirements (e.g., military service or payment of certain taxes) and the cases of moralistic or paternalistic requirements that do not mirror the requirements of objective morality. If there is no moral duty to *obey* in such cases, action contrary to law may routinely be morally acceptable.

This implies, of course, that there is a significant difference between the practical stances of a *philosophical* anarchist – who denies the duty to obey but in no way sanctions routine legal nonconformity, active resistance, or revolution – and a *political* anarchist committed to the overthrow of existing states (and to the ultimate replacement of states with alternative forms of social

---

5 More specifically, we should (normally) perform as required or forbidden by law when (a) the acts in question are also required or forbidden by natural morality; (b) the acts are of general types that are not naturally required or forbidden, but where context makes them so (as, e.g., in consequence of a scheme of coordination, such as is accomplished by some traffic laws); (c) natural morality leaves open the detailed content of some moral duty, which can legitimately be filled out by agreement or social conventions (as might be true of, e.g., the duties relating to property or contracts); (d) we have good moral reason of a weaker (i.e., nonduty) sort so to act and no more weighty reasons to do otherwise.

organization). Wellman, however, denies that the philosophical anarchist is entitled to claim such a difference in practical stance, arguing that "it is very difficult simultaneously to endorse philosophical anarchism without also committing oneself to political anarchism" (Chapter 1). Where states coerce us without having any special right to our obedience (like masters coercing their slaves), they are wronging us and giving us good moral reasons to actively resist the state (in order to prevent this wrongdoing, just as we should actively resist slavery). Philosophical anarchists should be political anarchists – an implication sufficiently unpalatable, Wellman believes, that it will discredit philosophical anarchism.

There are, however, several ways that philosophical anarchists can forcefully resist Wellman's efforts to put the bricks and bottles in their hands. My own preferred route is avowedly Lockean and involves affirming the natural right of all persons to enforce morality (by coercion, if necessary). If persons do, indeed, have such a right, then so do those officials who employ the institutions of law and government to secure our moral rights. Those officials wrong the people over whom they exercise such power primarily only in coercively preventing rival enforcement (attempts at which are usually infrequent) and in extending the law's requirements beyond those actions that we also have independent moral reasons to perform. These wrongs, while serious, are nothing like the systematic wrong that would be done were all state coercion wrongful (and are nothing like the wrongs done by a master to a slave). And they seem to me to be wrongs that are, in normal circumstances in decent states, insufficiently serious to justify risking the widespread misery and social upheaval that could be expected to flow from active or revolutionary resistance to the state (or to states generally). This line of argument, notice, allows the philosophical anarchist to embrace the commonsense judgment that states generally do no serious moral wrong in threatening and punishing murderers and rapists. Alternatively (and also plausibly), the philosophical anarchist could hold that we have no duty to oppose wrongs to others unless those others clearly want or request such opposition (or, perhaps, unless they *would* want or request it if they were reasonably enlightened). Even if the state is in fact wronging those it coerces, then, if the coerced prefer such wrongs to possible revolution or civil war (or if they would, reasonably enlightened, still have such preferences) – as seems likely – we stand under no moral duty to break out the bombs. Philosophical anarchists have these (and other) means available to dissociate themselves from their bomb-throwing anarchist relatives.

As I have indicated already, I am prepared to grant (at least *arguendo*) all that is said about the accomplishments of modern states and modern legal systems – about their importance (or even their necessity) for the efficient provision of a (relatively) secure environment under the rule of law; about their importance (or even their necessity) for solving the coordination and assurance problems that would plague even a relatively benign social condition without government and law; about their consequent importance (or even their necessity) for the provision of a wide range of other public goods. That granted, however, it must surely be granted as well that all of this is not bought without obvious costs. I refer here not only to the necessary costs (referred to by Wellman) in independence and self-government. States and legal systems can make all these good things possible only by concentrating enormous power, and concentrated enormous power is an enormously dangerous thing. The modern state's moral record is far from exemplary. It has made possible (and depressingly frequent) slaughter, terror, persecution, injustice, and manipulation on a scale that would be otherwise unimaginable. Even decent or reasonably just states – our principal concern here – have, despite their virtues, usually done great wrongs in their pasts, and they continue to do impressive jobs of solidifying social (ethnic, religious, racial) hierarchies, of institutionalizing condescending and moralizing attitudes, of threatening and controlling persons and nations outside their territories, and so on. None of this is news; even the best states and legal systems with which we are familiar are far from unqualified moral blessings.

But suppose this were not so. Suppose some (or all) states and legal systems were simply unqualifiedly good things to have in the world. Even in that case, I believe, it would not follow that each person had a moral duty to obey and support that state in whose claimed territories she happened to be born or reside. The claims of states to their territories (and to their consequent authority over those within those territories) are not morally unchallengeable.[6] The claims of rival would-be providers of the services provided by established governments are not morally dismissible without argument. The (unusual) values of those who favor independence and self-provision over subjection to some state (and to receipt of the benefits that state provides) are not morally inconsiderable simply because they are unusual. But even forgetting such challenges, the argument for a duty to obey remains feeble. Imagine that some organization, like an enormously expanded and impossibly efficient Oxfam, was an unqualified good thing, making possible decent lives for many millions who would otherwise live briefly and die horribly in abject poverty. Is there a moral duty to give to (this imagined version of) Oxfam? However much inclined we might ourselves be to give to others through such an organization, it seems clear to me that there can be no *duty* to do so. Oxfam's work is charity; and I can surely be a model of charity by working tirelessly myself (rather than just giving money) to help many others, or by giving (more) money instead to other worthy (but, perhaps, less efficient) charitable organizations.

But the state is different, the argument goes. Only the state can do the good it does, and the good it does is essential to decent lives for anyone. Even if the state *is* different in this way, though, it simply does not follow that only *this* state, with *these* officials, and *this* organization, making its morally arbitrary (and no doubt historically unjust) claim to *this* territory can do the good in question. We need not choose (as Wellman encourages us to) between *this* state, with the duty of obedience with which it attempts to bind us, and the chaos of a nonpolitical state of nature. I can instead choose to live in this state while recognizing it for what it

---

6 See my "On the Territorial Rights of States" in *Philosophical Issues* 11 (2001) (Supplement to *Nous*) (*Social, Political, and Legal Philosophy*, ed. E. Sosa and E. Villanueva).

is – an historically contingent organization that has amassed its enormous power by frequently dubious means (and has regularly abused that power), in the process doing considerable good and averting considerable evil – and while trying my best to treat others well and to advance good ends as morality mandates. I can choose to contract or cooperate with others, undertaking the duties of a willing promiser or cooperator; or I can keep to myself and let others exclude me from their schemes (including their political schemes, with the goods those provide) as best they can. If I love my state (or desire for other reasons a closer association with it), I can always freely choose to bind myself to it. If I hate my state, I may leave it in search of better (should that be possible). Or I may choose to live where I am as only a "citizen of the world," bound to no polity, but only to discharge those moral duties that each person owes naturally to every other. Others may, of course, find this kind of domestic detachment unattractive or threatening. They are entitled to avoid those who display it (insofar as this is consistent with their moral duties), and that fact, like the fact of the attractive goods that states can supply to their members, provides a strong and perfectly legitimate incentive for persons to sign on. States can plainly do far more than they do to encourage voluntary membership – and they would, in my view, have strong reason to do more were more people to openly embrace philosophical anarchism. But regardless of the truth of that speculation, another truth seems to me fundamental: However powerful and central to our lives state and political community may be, they can legitimately do no more to us without our consent than could the persons who created and empowered them. And those persons were bound always to respect the rights to autonomy and nonaggression that all enjoy.

Our political lives undoubtedly require more thought and judgment once we rid ourselves of the illusion that we are bound by a nonvoluntary, general moral duty to obey the law. But the arguments demand that we do so. As we have seen, the mere necessity of the state, even if we accept it, cannot by itself suffice to *locate* authority claims (or correlative claims of a duty to obey). Nor can the mere *salience* of existing institutions and officials. And our natural moral duties, properly understood, cannot serve to direct our moral attention first and foremost to the local. If that is correct, then the denial of a general moral duty of domestic legal obedience can perfectly well be maintained even in conjunction with the acceptance of standard claims about the importance or necessity of states and legal systems to the provision of familiar public goods. When this last point is joined to the failure of the three families of theories purporting to justify claims of a moral duty to obey, our conclusion follows. For most persons in most contemporary states, the answer to the question "Is there a duty to obey the law?" is "no."

Index

CPSIA information can be obtained
at www.ICGtesting.com
Printed in the USA
FSHW011335190821
84180FS

9 780521 537841